# Cambridge Elements

**Elements in Comparative Political Theory**
edited by
Leigh K. Jenco
*London School of Economics*

# REIMAGINING RADICAL DEMOCRACY IN THE GLOBAL SOUTH

## *Emerging Paradigms from Colombia and Türkiye*

Kaan Ağartan
*Framingham State University*
Camilo Tamayo Gomez
*The University of Huddersfield*

CAMBRIDGE
UNIVERSITY PRESS

Shaftesbury Road, Cambridge CB2 8EA, United Kingdom

One Liberty Plaza, 20th Floor, New York, NY 10006, USA

477 Williamstown Road, Port Melbourne, VIC 3207, Australia

314–321, 3rd Floor, Plot 3, Splendor Forum, Jasola District Centre, New Delhi – 110025, India

103 Penang Road, #05–06/07, Visioncrest Commercial, Singapore 238467

Cambridge University Press is part of Cambridge University Press & Assessment, a department of the University of Cambridge.

We share the University's mission to contribute to society through the pursuit of education, learning and research at the highest international levels of excellence.

www.cambridge.org
Information on this title: www.cambridge.org/9781009498500

DOI: 10.1017/9781009498517



When citing this work, please include a reference to the DOI 10.1017/9781009498517

First published 2024

*A catalogue record for this publication is available from the British Library*

ISBN 978-1-009-49850-0 Hardback
ISBN 978-1-009-49852-4 Paperback
ISSN 2633-3597 (online)
ISSN 2633-3589 (print)

# Reimagining Radical Democracy in the Global South

## Emerging Paradigms from Colombia and Türkiye

Elements in Comparative Political Theory

DOI: 10.1017/9781009498517
First published online: November 2024

---

Kaan Ağartan
*Framingham State University*

Camilo Tamayo Gomez
*The University of Huddersfield*

**Author for correspondence:** Kaan Ağartan, kagartan@framingham.edu

**Abstract:** Radical democracy informs contemporary social movements both as critique of existing liberal democratic social orders and as inspiration for collective action to challenge power structures. However, existing approaches on the relationship between radical democracy and social movements often truncate complex sociopolitical issues, constraining political imagination and stifling 'truly radical' alternatives. This Element offers an analysis of contemporary social movements in Colombia and Türkiye to show the limits and potential of radical democracy to reimagine new expressions of citizenship and non-capitalist alternatives. It argues that there is a mismatch between the radical democratic paradigm as it is formulated within Eurocentric purview, and the ways it has been articulated and practised by anti-austerity and pro-democracy movements of the twenty-first century. This Element proposes that radical democracy should be rethought in light of novel forms of political activism and visions emerging from these social movements as a response to the failures of liberal democracy.

**Keywords:** radical democracy and social movements, environmental citizenship, commoning, Türkiye, Colombia



ISBNs: 9781009498500 (HB), 9781009498524 (PB), 9781009498517 (OC)
ISSNs: 2633-3597 (online), 2633-3589 (print)

# Contents

# 1 Radical Democracy and Social Movements: Some Introductory Thoughts

In Colombia, growing social discontent due to the failure in establishing a lasting peace following the official ceasefire between the government and the FARC in 2016 was exacerbated by economic crises, deepening inequality and corruption in recent years. As a result, thousands of Colombians took to the streets in 2019 and again in 2021 to protest austerity measures and police violence. Just several years earlier, in a different part of the world, in Türkiye, a handful of environmentalists were joined by thousands when the neoliberal Islamist government attempted to demolish Gezi Park, one of the last remaining green areas in the heart of Istanbul, to build a high-end shopping mall catering to the consumption frenzy under global capitalism.

These two seemingly unrelated cases of social mobilisation had at least one thing in common, even if it was not immediately obvious to the naked eye: a yearning for a new social contract, a new mode of citizenship that acknowledged, respected and responded to the diverse demands from different sectors of the society. Both societies were in anticipation for a steady transition into a more inclusive and harmonious democratic social order yet were deeply frustrated with the inability of their respective governments to deliver on these promises. The 'unconventional' organisational methods (horizontal, non-hierarchical, direct, participatory, etc.) and repertoires of action (encampments, assemblies, and other forms of activism as everyday life) that emerged from the protests in both cases went beyond mere expressions of discontent, but practically turned the public space into sites of solidarity through enactments of civil disobedience that nurtured aspirations for a radically new society.

These two examples – along with numerous other anti-austerity and pro-democracy movements of the twenty-first century – stand testament that 'radical democracy' has become an inspiration shaping the political vision and horizon of contemporary social movements. Indeed, practices, values and organisational forms of radical democracy emerging from these movements diverged from the methods, principles and institutions of representative liberal democracy, primarily because of the concrete, pragmatic and almost always non-capitalist solutions they offered for the immediate needs of their communities (such as kitchens, infirmaries, vegetable gardens, childcare centres and so on) inflicted by neoliberalism. These radical and novel enactments then became the operating mode of diverse groups collaborating and collectively taking decisions in the course of contentious politics. This particular mode of collective mobilisation based on horizontalism, autonomy, and non-representative political action without a hierarchical structure or leadership turned radical democracy into a theoretical and practical guide to 'comprehend today's form of protest as a critique of the current shape of modern democratic order' (Volk, 2021: 438) rather than a corrective to and rectification of the existing system.

If we define politics as the regulation of conflict within a society and among societies for the accomplishment of collective goals, then radical democracy is indeed a novel form in which political thought can be expressed through innovative ideas and unstated biases that in turn drive collective political conduct (Freeden, 2003; Trend, 1996a). We identify three modalities through which radical democracy entwines with such political conduct: first off, radical democracy can be seen as an open-ended struggle, a conflictual and contestatory set of political practices taking place in different realms of civil society (Matijasevich, 2019: 2). Radical democratic ideas stimulate political thought by offering new frameworks to re-imagine deliberation and communal participation in which a citizen-led direct action can flourish. Second, radical democracy encompasses a distinct repertoire of political practices that contest the boundaries of 'the political' in double sense: first, by developing new agendas and topics that come to be considered as 'political', and second, by focusing on the formation of new subjectivities in and through collective mobilisation (Barnett & Low, 2009). As such, the notion of radical democracy activates new political ideas and symbols through which citizens and social movements can reformulate the parameters of their collective political action (Tønder & Thomassen, 2005). And finally, radical democracy offers important practical and theoretical ways for rethinking the degree to which deliberation, participation, and contestation contend with the problem of representation. Here the radical democratic paradigm operates under the assumption that the acknowledgement of new 'localities' as sites of direct political action (a square, neighbourhood park, squat house, and so forth) and innovative thought (in our case, novel conceptions of citizenship and socio-economic order) would stimulate better communal governance by virtue of being closer to people's everyday concerns. Therefore, while radical democracy recognises representation as an irreducible aspect of any viable, pluralistic model of democracy, it nevertheless encourages the decentralisation of decision-making and political participation, and thus moving beyond the predominant formal and spatial framings of democracy (Barnett & Low, 2009; Newman, 2016).

It is these novelties in radical democracy that unleash the 'constitutive power' inherent in contemporary social movements. According to Kalyvas (2005) and Del Lucchese (2016), this particular form of power is the creative and productive capacity of people to constitute their own collective forms of political life, and not merely participating in those that are given. Contentious politics with a radical democratic orientation not only aims to disrupt an existing order that perpetuates patterns of social inequality, power imbalance or exclusion/marginalisation, but also sets the stage for 'those who have no part' to begin to claim their part (Rancière, 1999: 9). It engenders a 'constitutive disruption' in which agents of political action 'step out' of their assigned identities or expected functions (as workers, students, middle classes, etc.), and develop new political subjectivities with contingent, if volatile, interests and demands (Matijasevich, 2019: 6–11). As such, radical democracy paves the way for a unique type of citizenry to emerge 'through successful democratic political activism, where citizens see their engagements as contributing to their own and societies' self-constitution' (Dahlberg, 2013). In other words, the radical democratic character of contemporary social movements possesses the constitutive power to replace an old, oppressive, dysfunctional social order associated with representative democracy with a collectively imagined one that re-appropriates, re-invents, and radicalises democracy (Celikates, 2021: 129–130).

*Reimagining Radical Democracy in the Global South* is a call for critically rethinking the ways through which 'radical democracy-as-theory' can (and ought to) respond to the expectations of, and demands from, 'radical democracy-as-social movement'. In other words, we aim to demonstrate that contemporary social movements – especially those in non-European contexts – oblige the radical democratic paradigm to descend from a purely abstract level of 'contemplating' democracy to the act of 'practising' it, all the while revealing some significant shortcomings of the paradigm. We further argue that while the radical democratic paradigm rightly points out the need for revitalising democracy and empowering citizens through an expansive understanding of the political beyond the formal institutions and practices of liberal democracy, it fails to interpret the ways contemporary social movements have engendered novel and innovative forms of egalitarian self-governance in everyday social interactions.

As we hope to substantiate in the following pages, our cases of Colombia and Türkiye allow us to detect a tendency in the radical democratic paradigm: reproducing Western ideas about how democracy can operate in a globalised world, while ignoring more inclusive and diverse non-Western approaches to reimagine the future of liberal democracy as a cosmopolitan project. The main issue here is that radical democracy as a theoretical concept has not matured to embrace alternative ways of engaging in egalitarian and emancipatory politics outside Western contexts (Tambakaki, 2019). As Robinson and Tormey assert in their critique of Laclau and Mouffe's work:

> the perspectival 'conditions of possibility' identified by Laclau and Mouffe with the 'human condition' turn out to be parochially metropolitan, arising primarily in urbanised societies at the core of the world system. In a typically Eurocentric gesture, this European particularity is then 'globalised', identified

> with humanity as such. Indigenous perspectives are thus elided, declared in advance to be impossible and silenced within a discourse which treats metropolitan 'reason' as universal. (Robinson & Tormey, 2009: 144)

Put differently, the dominant paradigms of radical democracy seemed to be still primarily locked within a set of epistemological assumptions from the Global North, and as such fall short in igniting its full radical potential in the perspectives, cosmologies, practices, and imaginaries of the non-Western 'other' (Conway & Singh, 2011). One of the major tasks of *Reimagining Radical Democracy in the Global South* is, then, to offer an insight into how radical democracy as theory fails to recognise – let alone guide – ongoing novel processes of political disruption and emerging egalitarian visions that have been nurtured by social movements in the non-core regions of the capitalist world.

It is important for us to spell out from the outset that we do not regard our endeavour as a mere academic exercise or otherwise an apolitical effort. We believe that rethinking and recalibrating radical democracy through the cases of Colombia and Türkiye is a vital step to challenge prevailing power dynamics and to contribute to the efforts for a more inclusive distribution of social, political, and economic resources. By embracing the term's complexity, we hope to offer a renewed understanding of radical democracy that can disrupt existing power imbalances, catalyse new types of social contracts, and unleash radical democracy's transformative potential. Our goal is to effectively challenge the dominance of liberal democratic ideas and practices, and to contribute to past, current and future efforts to redress inequalities and injustices.

*Reimagining Radical Democracy in the Global South* is organised as follows: The next section argues that radical democracy as employed in existing paradigms of radical democracy fails to grasp two realities on the ground: (1) how contemporary social movements have produced new forms of citizenship experiences which could build the foundations of new social contracts that transcend classical state-citizen models, and (2) how new social orders were prefigured beyond merely an updated form of socialism in which the commodification of life is not at the centre of social and economic relations. The following two sections flesh out each of these 'blind spots' respectively. Section 3 takes on the task by focusing on how ecological social movements in Colombia are exercising new dimensions of environmental citizenship to provide useful insights into connecting crucial ecological concerns with alternative (and enhanced) conceptualisations of radical democracy. The section showcases different phases of environmental activism in recent decades and how novel types of collective action shape the relationship between humanity and the environment from a posthumanistic perspective. In Section 4 we shift our attention to the second blind spot by way of focusing on the

2013 Gezi Park protests and their aftermath in Türkiye. The section highlights how daily practices of radical democracy in park forums and other urban sites have motivated and mobilised activists to develop a new sense of urban citizenship around the concept of the 'common'. We argue that everyday activism in public forums, neighbourhood solidarities and squat houses became 'rehearsals' in building a new collectivity in response to the docile consumer-subject-citizen model imposed by the neoliberal Islamist government. In Section 5 we reiterate the main claim in the Element that there exists a mismatch between the concept/theory of radical democracy as currently formulated in the literature and the ways through which it is articulated in contentious politics in non-European contexts. After revisiting how political activism and non-capitalist visions in Colombia and Türkiye challenged existing conceptual frameworks in the radical democratic theory, we emphasise the need for a more comprehensive articulation of radical democracy beyond the narrow epistemological canvas of the Global North.

## 2 Radical Democracy as Incomplete Praxis: A Critique of Existing Paradigms

At its core, radical democracy, as both theory and practice, aims to challenge existing power structures, and champions alternative forms of citizen participation and political governance. As such, it carries a potential to inform and shape contemporary social movements both as a critique of existing liberal democratic social order (especially the latter's inability to tackle processes that deepen inequality and political apathy among citizens) and as an actual venture to replace it. However, as we demonstrate herein, in both its epistemological and activist outlooks, radical democracy has been marred with a tendency to reduce complex sociopolitical issues which, to date, constrained sociopolitical imagination and stifled 'truly alternative' viewpoints.

We believe that in order to uncover and activate the real transformative power of radical democracy as a concept and a political inspiration/guide/strategy, it is imperative to recognise and transcend its inherent limitations. More specifically, radical democracy needs to grasp two realities on the ground which it has failed to address adequately: (1) contemporary social movements have produced new forms of citizenship experiences which could build the foundations of a new social contract beyond the classical state-citizen model, and (2) contemporary social movements have imagined, developed and implemented non-capitalist practices that transcended a merely updated form of socialism. We believe that these two major 'blind spots' within the literature on radical democracy prevented it from developing a more comprehensive interpretation of contemporary social movements, and hence eclipsed its capacity to effectively guide them.

## 2.1 Revisiting the Blind Spots of Radical Democracy – I: The Ideological/Political Dimension

The first of the blind spots in radical democratic theory appears in what we call 'ideological/political dimension'. It is in this dimension that radical democratic theory builds upon the inclusive, participatory, and contestatory qualities of liberal democracy, encouraging new ways of thinking about diversity, liberty, freedom, and civic responsibility. In other words, it embraces and furthers the notion of 'difference' to catalyse the rebirth of liberal democracy from within a more radically egalitarian framework (Mouffe, 2000, 2005). The core and animating ideology of radical democracy is thus democratic pluralism: broadening and extending practices of self-government to more spheres of social life and to more diverse groups (Forst, 2017; Popp-Madsen, 2022).

This particular emphasis in radical democratic theory is a reflection of post-Marxism's dispute with orthodox interpretations of Marxism on the primacy of material base over ideational superstructure (Freeden, 2003; Tambakaki, 2019). For post-Marxists, one of the fundamental functions of ideology is the production of social order. Unlike more rigid social structures, practices of democracy are discursive in that they are human, optional, and contingent articulations of how we should understand society (Popp-Madsen, 2022). As such, social orders are not given, but socially constructed and articulated. Thus, the notion of radical democracy is a progressive extension of the core liberal democratic notions of liberty, rationality, freedom, and equality; underscoring that democracy is always a reflexive, unfinished, and contested ideological sociopolitical process (Dahlberg & Siapera, 2007; Pettit, 2013).

Prominent scholars of radical democracy, first and foremost Ernesto Laclau and Chantal Mouffe, have argued that the vagueness of social order requires the construction of novel signifiers to critique contemporary liberal democracy (Laclau, 2005; Mouffe, 2018; also see Brown, 2019). Here, the notion of radical democracy itself becomes an innovative signifier that represents the need to challenge neoliberal and neoconservative concepts of democracy and to recognise difference as a crucial element to expand liberal democracy against the rise for authoritarianism, right-wing populism, totalitarianism, and elitist technocracy (Mouffe, 2013; Volk, 2021). In other words, radical democracy carries an inherent assumption that there exist repressive and unequal power relations in social structures that need to be exposed, challenged, and transformed (Kioupkiolis & Katsambekis, 2014; Mouffe, 2013, 2018).

Theorised as such, radical democracy rests on certain pillars. First and foremost, it seeks to establish the equivalence of particular demands and identities in line with the liberal democratic values of freedom, equality, and solidarity against all forms of domination and injustice based particularly on sexuality, gender, race, religion or environmental concerns. Second, the articulation of these demands is predicated on an institutional infrastructure (rule of law, accountability, party politics, rights, etc.) through which political agencies engage with each other as well as with the state, in the process of developing particular political subjectivities. Finally, this interaction – which is often seen as agonistic and expected to evolve into a populist, hegemonic form to establish a unified front in the struggle for emancipation – is projected to pave the way for the diffusion of core values of liberal democracy into the state and market domains and institutions. As such, the worldview of radical democracy, despite its radical-ness, remains within the parameters of existing liberal social order (Howarth & Roussos, 2022).

This theoretical architecture no doubt informs radical democracy's political outlook and potential, which is especially relevant to understanding its relation to contemporary social movements. This is particularly true since radical democracy encourages the emergence of informed, structured participatory discussions, and open decision-making processes as central aspects of democratic theory (Barnett & Low, 2009) which have been central to these movements. It implies an active role for social movements and citizens in all aspects of political decision-making and the extension of democratic norms in everyday activities. Thus, radical democracy as actual political practice contributes to a broader democratic culture through deepening open deliberation and collective political action (Calhoun, 1992; Habermas, 1994, 1997) and promoting creative political imagination (Hardt & Negri, 2017; Popp-Madsen, 2022). This is why almost all anti-austerity and pro-democracy movements of the early twenty-first century adopted inclusive, participatory, deliberative, and agonistic qualities of radical democracy at the centre of their activism. The radical democratic framework they were inspired from helped activists comprehend their actions (deliberation, communal participation and the like) as a path to citizen-led collective action for real social change.

While radical democracy as a theoretical guide inspires social movements, grassroots organisations and other groups engaging in contentious politics, the concept itself hinges on an old, if not obsolete, iteration of politics – one that centres 'political citizenship'. This is where we detect a disconnect between theory and its political prospects and potential, especially from the perspective of social movements. More specifically, radical democracy as a concept rests on the conventional interpretation of political citizenship (defined by rights and representation which are also fundamental pillars of liberal democracy) in its relation to different social movements. While it sees these movements primarily as efforts for recognition and acceptance by the state, it ignores novel epistemologies that emerge from these movements' prefigurative activism and other forms of political practice – a unique practice that opens the way for reimagining social contract around different political subjectivities, not in isolation within each movement but collectively and in tandem with others.

To be sure, these movements and grassroots mobilisations have often aspired to be recognised by the state and other agents of the political authority based on particular sociopolitical identities they carry. Yet they have not done this simply to be regarded (and treated) as autonomous, self-enclosed groups defined solely by these very identities in a multicultural context. Their activism and collaboration with each other often had a transformative impact on themselves and on the way through which they articulated their 'struggle' in discourse and in action. The type of activism they engaged in reveals a complex, dynamic and multifaceted – if not 'fluid' – idea of citizenship as a core operative of a renewed social contract in contemporary times. Even when Laclau and Mouffe offer a reconceptualisation of the citizen in which the political subjectification of the individual is not compartmentalised as a rigid constituent of an interest group, and each individual belongs to numerous overlapping groups and multiple intersecting identities rather than being a fixed and universal subject (Trend, 1996a: 15), they fail to note how a novel political identity emerges around a 'common concern' from a variety of democratic demands – a condition that cannot be fully captured by the concept of 'hegemony' (Mouffe, 1996: 24). What the theory of radical democracy ultimately fails to address, in our opinion, is to take this complexity into account and instead get stuck with a narrow definition of political citizenship (i.e., making claims of identity expression based on race, ethnicity, sex, gender identity, etc.) as the primary ground for social movements. This is despite the theory's self-proclaimed premise that 'citizenship is not just one identity among others [but an] articulating principle' and 'to be a citizen is to recognize the authority of [political] principles and the rules in which they are embodied' (Mouffe, 1993: 84, 65). Put differently, the radical democratic epistemology does not embrace 'the idea that politics can be imagined outside the state; that politics can incorporate a logic different to that of the state [. . .] The sovereign state is not the only site of political projects, and there is indeed the possibility of the construction of autonomous political spaces which do not refer to the state and its representative channels' (Newman, 2014: 98–99). It is also silent when subordinated groups in society actually get 'included' through formal mechanisms of representation (what Dhaliwal calls 'oppressive inclusion') without disturbing or destabilising the unequal relationships at the core of the existing social contract (Dhaliwal, 1996: 44).

This blind spot in the theory leads to an inaccurate portrayal of (or implicit assumption about) activists as oscillating between two political dead-ends: they are depicted either as 'resigning from' traditional politics (often seen as 'political apathy' on the part of citizens) or 'playing by the rules of the game' which means taking for granted individual rights and freedoms as officially recognised and protected by the state, and utilising the tools of liberal democracy to gain recognition (e.g., electoral processes to pursue the idea of democratic governance). As a result, radical democracy cannot grasp the extent to which actual exercise of political power through creative activism empowered social movements to entertain alternative citizenship imaginaries. More specifically, instead of seeking or working through a hegemonic composition to articulate their demands, these movements prefigured and actually built (even if temporarily) a new solidaristic order around the idea of the 'common' through autonomous, bottom-up, non-hierarchical organising and everyday activism in squares, occupied parks, squat houses, and others. More importantly, this modality of politics produced a novel political subjectivity and democratic imaginary that inhabited such an order. While engaging in such politics, separate movements could unite – even if loosely and temporarily – around common ideals, values and practices because they could see the core of their problems crystallising under the same condition: neoliberalism. When they assembled in squares, parks, neighbourhoods and other urban spaces, they could reimagine their activism as a part of a mutual struggle against a common enemy. Their political subjectivities and the emerging democratic imaginaries were all conditioned by the realisation of the commonality in their separate struggles which not only aimed to get recognised as an identity group but to radically transform the existing social order to effect real social change.

It is clear that this rich political experience which includes both (1) the dynamics that successfully brought different social groups and their demands into the fold not under a hierarchical structure of hegemony but around a horizontal, solidaristic multitude, and (2) contradictions that emerged within this multitude, leading to its eventual unravelling almost everywhere in the world, cannot be captured by a narrow definition of 'political citizenship' around recognition and chain of equivalence to which the radical democratic paradigm subscribes. It would be wrong to assume that the recognition of difference and achieving plurality can automatically create the conditions of radical democracy (Matijasevich, 2019). More importantly, radical democracy as currently defined cannot offer robust tools, nor can it formulate new frameworks to understand (let alone guide) the 'rehearsals' of the new social contract that contemporary social movements prefigure.

Recounting the trajectory of political citizenship may be instructive here. In its most conventional form, citizenship is defined as a particular sociopolitical connection among a group of people around a special type of social contract: it is 'a continuing series of transactions between persons and agents of a given state in which each has enforceable rights and obligations uniquely by virtue of (1) the person's membership in a exclusive category, the native – born plus the naturalised and; (2) the agent's relation to the state rather than any other authority the agent may enjoy' (Tilly, 1995: 8). Stevenson argues that the category of citizenship is 'more often thought to be about membership, belonging, rights and obligations. In institutional terms the terrain of citizenship is usually marked out by abstract legal definitions as to who is to be included and excluded from the political community' (Stevenson, 2003: 4). Nevertheless, scholars as diverse as Castells (2006), Bauman (2007), Beck (2002), Plummer (2003), Croucher (2004), Held (2004), Hermes (2006), Sassen (2007), and Vertovec (2009) agree that this traditional meaning of citizenship no longer reflects the reality on the ground. In the past decades a wide range of conceptualisations such as 'global citizenship' (Falk, 1994), 'media citizenship' (Castells, 1997), 'cultural citizenship' (Stevenson, 2003), 'intimate citizenship' (Plummer, 2003), 'cosmopolitan citizenship' (Held, 2004), 'ecological citizenship' (Dobson, 2004), 'transnational citizenship' (Vertovec, 2009), or 'transgendering citizenship' (Monro, 2012), among others, have emerged as ways of expressing a wealth of new individual and collective experiences through which the traditional definitions of rights, duties, and responsibilities have been challenged.

On the other side of the coin of the debate on citizenship is the transformation of the nation-state. Scholars including Beck (2002), Žižek (2019), and Fraser (2022) have argued that the nation-state is morphing into a type of political organisation or apparatus involving multiple and overlapping jurisdictions, set of identities, political contracts, types of capitalism, and social orders that are no longer really contained by borders. For those scholars, the traditional function of the nation-state to define a sense of belonging with one territory, in part for its political and symbolic centrality, is now in dispute with different forms of social, economic, and citizen experience. In the same vein, Croucher (2004) and Zuboff (2019) established that the declining relevance of the state is considered an indicator of globalisation, showcasing novel forms of belonging, surveillance, capitalism, and citizenship connected to identities, political subjectivities, or individual experiences.

These new developments push us to reformulate the definition of radical democracy in which the conventional understanding of political citizenship (which solely rests on recognition of demands and identities, and the expansion of the liberal democratic domain without fundamentally changing the latter's institutional infrastructure) can no longer be the main pivot of democratic experience. And yet, while radical democratic epistemology and practice is conceived in opposition to liberal democracy, it is still inherently tied to a framework that centres the state as the primary – if not only – political canvas within which the values of diversity, liberty, freedom, and civic responsibility can be reinvigorated. In fact, radical democracy's aim is not 'to renounce liberal democratic ideology, but on the contrary to deepen and extend it in the direction of a radical and plural democracy' (Laclau & Mouffe, 1985). This is why, we believe, that radical democratic paradigm fails in capturing the possibility of alternative political social orders as imagined and partially emerged in contemporary social movements, not only during street protests but also in square occupations, park assemblies, neighbourhood solidarities and squat houses. As we aim to demonstrate through the examples of social movements in Türkiye and Colombia, this particular blind spot in the paradigm prevents it from possessing the analytical tools to explain the potentials and failures of political mobilisation to achieve real social change and establish novel social contracts. Our cases, we believe, will help reveal these shortcomings in radical democracy especially when the state does not guarantee the best practices/possibilities for citizenship and when citizenship claims by social movements go beyond recognition by state authority.

## 2.2 Revisiting the Blind Spots of Radical Democracy – II: The Political Economy Dimension

The second 'blind spot' in the radical democratic paradigm as we see it is the latter's failure in conceptualising capitalism as a comprehensive social order and, by extension, in interpreting contemporary developments in capitalism as manifestations of a deep crisis in that very order. Put differently, radical democracy has been unable to connect the sociocultural and political transformations that underlie the 'identity impulses' of the 1960s and 1970s (Zaretsky, 1996) with the evolution of the capitalist world-system and with the ways capitalist dynamics/processes conditioned these transformations. As we will demonstrate later, this failure also resulted in the inability of the radical democratic theory in capturing the complexity of the emerging anti-capitalist epistemologies, visions, and everyday practices within contemporary social movements.

A diverse set of scholars ranging from Mason (2015) and Zuboff (2019) to Žižek (2018) and Burke (2022) has argued that contemporary capitalism is facing a triple crisis as it became financially unstable, environmentally unsustainable, and politically unpopular. According to Nancy Fraser (2020, 2022) the roots of this condition can be found in that capitalism is an institutionalised social order that not only operates in the economic realm, but also relies on background 'conditions of possibility' which include social reproduction, public power, nonhuman nature, and other 'forms of wealth that lie outside capital's official circuits but within its reach'. The current crisis, then, can be seen as a symptom of capitalism not being able to function as a self-sustaining social order. Having lost its capacity (not to mention its legitimacy) to organise processes of social reproduction as well as economic production and environmental sustainability, the capitalist social order is undermining the very conditions of its own survival.

Following Fraser's lead, we identify six manifestations of the crisis of capitalism as a social order (also see Burke, 2022; Ibrahim, 2021; Tambakaki, 2019; Valencia, 2018). First, the concentration of wealth in the hands of a few rich individuals has led to vast *economic disparities and rising inequality*, hindering social cohesion and upward social mobility. Second, unrestrained pursuit of economic gain through relentless commodification of natural life and resource extraction resulted in severe *environmental degradation*, the symptoms of which include climate change, deforestation, and pollution, undermining long-term ecological stability. Third, unregulated markets that harboured monopolistic practices, information imbalances, and externalities have led to *structural market failures,* harming individuals and communities, and requiring regulatory interventions that further depleted public resources – not to mention social solidarity (Mason, 2015). Fourth, *exploitative labour practices* have become the norm as corporations have prioritised cost reduction and profit maximisation, leading to poor working conditions, low wages, and labour rights violations, undermining the well-being of working communities, and perpetuating social injustice. Fifth, as the flagship of contemporary capitalism, the financial sector has prioritised quick gains and immediate profits over long-term investment and economic productivity, which has led to a vicious cycle of *short-termism and neglect of long-term innovation* at the expense of economic stability and social peace (Fraser, 2022). Finally, all these developments in contemporary capitalism have *eroded social cohesion*, cooperation, and solidarity, hampering communities' ability to address common challenges (Wolf, 2022). Put differently, capitalism's emphasis on individualism and consumption overshadowed the importance of social connections and community well-being.

As these 'morbid symptoms' became more profound and visible, new articulations have emerged to shed light on the complex and multifaceted ways capitalism operates through social, political, cultural, symbolic, and environmental dynamics. Notions such as Racial Capitalism (Robinson, 1983), Emotional Capitalism (Illouz, 2007), Post-Capitalism (Mason, 2015), Platform Capitalism (Srnicek, 2017) Disaster Capitalism (Klein, 2017), Gore Capitalism (Valencia, 2018), Surveillance Capitalism (Zuboff, 2019), Posthuman Capitalism (Ibrahim, 2021; Žižek, 2018), Cannibal Capitalism (Fraser,

2022), and Symbolic Capitalism (Al-Gharbi, 2023) came about to offer alternative lenses to diagnose various manifestations of the transformation the capitalist social order has been undergoing. It is possible to categorise these manifestations in two main constellations.

The first of these constellations is in regard to the challenges to the capitalist social order in the economic realm. Here we find various analyses highlighting the fact that recent advances in technology, such as automation and digitalisation of production facilitate the exchange of goods, services, and information that rely on network effects, data accumulation, and algorithmic control (Mason, 2015; Srnicek, 2017). These frameworks stress that a future socio-economic system has to go beyond capitalism, encouraging collaborative ways of production, shared resources, and non-market forms of exchange in the face of increasing labour precarity, lack of worker protections, and the concentration of power in the hands of platform owners, all of which exacerbate existing inequalities and exploitative labour practices.

Some other analyses in this constellation draw attention to the processes in which companies profit from the collection and analysis of personal data for targeted advertising and manipulation of consumer behaviour. Zuboff (2019), for instance, stresses that tech companies monetise surveillance data to optimise their products and services, creating new forms of power and control through manipulation, exploitation, and the erosion of individual autonomy. Others such as Klein (2017) highlight how capitalism has learned to exploit crises, disasters, and shocks to further economic gain through policies of privatisation, deregulation, and austerity measures, often at the expense of the most vulnerable populations, even when the very same crises opened possibilities to foster community resilience and solidarity.

The second constellation concerns the challenges to the capitalist social order in the symbolic/cultural/social realm. Here we find analyses such as Robinson's (1983), who argues that the organic connection between racism and capitalism has created novel socio-economic configurations in which capitalist exploitation and racial divisions and hierarchies become co-constitutive. Therefore, historical (and by extension contemporary) forms of racism perpetuated socio-economic as well as racial inequalities to maintain the hegemony of capitalism on both sides of the colour line.

A different body of work in this constellation emphasises how the rise of commodification and commercialisation of emotions in contemporary capitalist societies has made capitalism rely increasingly on the production, manipulation, and consumption of emotions as objects of economic value through advertising and branding, raising concerns about the instrumentalisation of human feelings for economic gain (Illouz, 2007; Konings, 2016; Pugh, 2008).

In the contemporary hyper-consumption era, individuals and groups pursue symbolic rewards including fame, influence, reputation, or social validation, usually through participation in social media networks, entertainment ecosystems, and digital platforms. Here the sociocultural realm becomes a site of accumulation of social status, recognition, and distinction through the production and consumption of symbolic goods and cultural capital (Al-Gharbi, 2023). The tension between symbolic rewards and material inequalities reinforces existing discrepancies in power structures, affecting social cohesion and potential for collective action in the society. This is also connected to the ways through which individuals experience individual and collective frustration when this promise of unceasing consumption cannot be achieved. The result is the emergence of what Valencia (2018) calls '*endriago* subjects' (subjects who utilise violence as a tool for empowerment and capital acquisition) and the legitimisation of the capitalist social order through necro-empowerment.

We believe that highlighting these two constellations of manifestations of the crisis in capitalism as a social order is important for it allows us to rethink the latter not simply in economic terms but as a dynamic (yet struggling) self-sustaining system with multiple dimensions, each of which shapes some aspect of human life and of the social contract between individuals, groups and the state. This is why these manifestations can be interpreted as both the crisis of the existing system and the labour pains of a new economic and sociocultural order beyond capitalism, neither of which can be detected by the analytical radar provided by the radical democratic theory. More importantly, a serious consideration of these constellations would reveal radical democracy's failure (but also its potential) as a theoretical tool and political praxis to imagine non-capitalist forms of existence that contemporary social movements have been prefiguring in the past two decades. While radical democratic theory refuses to reduce political conflict to class struggle, and while it aims to move beyond the capitalism-socialism dichotomy by highlighting the plurality and heterogeneity of 'new social movements', it still falls short of providing a more realistic description of what future politics may look like – one that is more aligned with reality on the ground where these very social movements happen. Indeed, what these movements have been experimenting with recently cannot be reduced to socialism – even a revised, reformed type of socialism – that the theoreticians of radical democracy present as the main, and in some cases, the only real 'radical' alternative to capitalism (Fraser, 2022; Mason, 2015).

We argue that this shortcoming is due to the theory's oversimplification of the complexities of the capitalist social order (its contradictions as well as its capacity to transform itself) and its under-theorisation of non-capitalist alternatives. This is mostly due to the fact that Laclau and Mouffe, along with other prominent radical democratic theorists, hastily discarded the notion of mode of production and anything related to political economy in favour of discourse as an interpretive framework to explain social change and structural transformation (Rey-Araújo, 2021: 39). In their effort to offer a more complex definition of antagonism as the motor of radical democracy they sought to diminish the role of capitalist relations of production and class struggle to emphasise the primacy of the political shaped by the 'identity' of the worker outside the realm of work (Rey-Araújo, 2021: 41). The failure to incorporate a comprehensive analysis of capitalism and its dynamics into the theory of radical democracy prevents the latter from accurately interpreting novel non-capitalist forms of social reproduction and conditions of existence in contemporary social movements. In other words, the theory of radical democracy fails to pay sufficient attention to the ways social conflict disturbs existing social orders but also creates new ones.

As the Turkish and Colombian cases demonstrate, the social movements of the twenty-first century were aware of the inadequacy of any model reminiscent of socialism and have already been building – using Wright's (2010) apt definition – 'real utopias' through prefiguring alternative social orders with their everyday activism. One set of such everyday activisms that emerged in the face of capitalism's imminent crisis includes social co-production (cooperatives, community gardens, and others), self-organising (rejecting corporate models in favour of worker ownership, collective management), commoning practices (re-appropriation of privatised material and immaterial resources in favour of the community control and ownership), mutual aid and support networks that provide basic social services (clinics, pharmacies, kitchens, food banks, libraries) and other socially beneficial, collective activities outside the realm of the market (Howarth & Roussos, 2022). These practices reject the capitalist logic (commodification, individualisation of responsibility, marketisation, competition, profit-oriented production) in production and social reproduction which open the ways to alternative vision of organising society.

This is important for our argument because political action by ordinary people does not necessarily require the formation of hegemony and establishment of leadership among a plurality of struggles, as radical democratic perspective would often presuppose. Rather, such politics 'typically occurs in the everyday settings familiar from their own lives, not in centralised movements seeking to take power' (Robinson & Tormey, 2009: 148). The political mobilisation of contemporary movements, too, unfolded without a leadership structure or a hegemonic organisation of multiple struggles under a common banner or signifier. In our view, the radical democratic paradigm can not capture this richness of political variation in contemporary social movements, especially with regard to how these groups actually join each other to create something collectively, from the barricades to squares, parks, squat houses and other sites of activism. In other words, the anti-capitalism of contemporary movements has been informed by collective prefigurative activism through which these movements have imagined a new world and strived to it one step at a time, without following a prescription. The anti-capitalist horizon of radical democracy, on the other hand, seems stuck with an abstract notion of 'communist horizon', even if this abstract notion was revised to accommodate the needs of the contemporary times. This is mainly due to the reason that for radical democratic theory, the main reference is still capitalism and its 'dislocatory power', that is its 'ruthless destruction of the bonds of tradition, local belonging, family and kinship structures' (Critchley, 2005: 223). It seems to us that in its goal to refuse the primacy of the 'universal subject', i.e., the proletariat, to reformulate emancipatory struggles in cultural terms, the theory limits its scope to fragmented struggles around identity. This tendency circumscribes its ability to consider the transformative power of smaller, even micro, practices of everyday life (i.e., 'being and doing in common') that are realised beyond the realm of the state. The theory, in other words, cannot imagine an emancipatory struggle that goes beyond making claims for state recognition and inclusion into a narrow definition of citizenship (Critchley, 2005: 226).

This is also why radical democracy falls short of guiding these movements as well. It cannot detect that contemporary social movements have been able to harmonise their many (and often conflicting) orientations, perspectives, practices, and aspirations, even if temporarily, irregularly and for brief periods. Just as the radical democratic paradigm of the 1970s and 1980s simply accepted the negligence of class in social movements which prevented the latter to develop a common structural critique (and a framework for emancipation) beyond their own oppressions, the radical democratic theory of our own times, too, fail to offer a more comprehensive understanding for and a critique of the complexities and novelties of the more recent wave of social movements, let alone steering them towards 'a broader political discourse that emphasises social justice, economic equality' as well as cultural tolerance and plurality (Omi & Winant, 1996: 164). The left of the past (especially in the West) had been plagued with 'little or no contact with grassroots organising efforts among inner-city working people, the poor, and the homeless [having] the luxury to contemplate "class struggle" in the abstract' (Marable, 1996: 151–152). Radical democracy of today seems to be reproducing this tendency when it imagines – or fails to imagine – anti-capitalist alternatives experimented by the contemporary social movements. These alternatives do not only or simply address the way capitalism perpetuates unequal conditions that the poor, the marginalised and the oppressed have to endure in various identity forms/

modalities (race, gender, sexuality, and so forth). They also imagine a new socio-economic order that rests on the common production, consumption, and distribution of the resources of the society.

All in all, despite its egalitarian vision and aspiration, we argue that radical democracy does not offer a fully developed model of redistribution as the core of the capitalist social order. In this framing, the emancipatory struggles anchored on cultural politics of identity are divorced from social politics of justice, solidarity, equality, and redistribution (Fraser, 1996: 194). In a sense, it goes too far in trying to move away from class as the primary/hegemonic identity that makes the theory incapable of embracing the complexity of capitalism as a social order in which difference and identity are formed. As a result, the radical democratic paradigm becomes incapable of comprehending (let alone guiding) anti-capitalist alternatives offered and experimented by contemporary social movements.

## 2.3 Unlocking Radical Democracy's Potential

To be sure, the theoretical universe of radical democracy is expansive and encompasses many different approaches. While various straits of thought within the radical democratic paradigm have indeed been incommunicable to the actual radical practices emerging from contemporary social movements, there have also been studies that embraced the elements of the necessary shift from liberal democracy to radical democracy by way of an engagement with the broader and more nuanced understanding of political and democratic concepts. Of notable importance are the works by Marchart (2007, Schwiertz (2021, 2022), Isin (2008), and Ní Mhurchú (2014) which explore a diverse set of notions and expand the concept of citizenship beyond its conventional meanings and iterations.

Utilising the concept of 'political difference', Marchart (2007) critiques the ontological assumptions of liberal democracy, which tend to obscure the inherent antagonism and contingency within the political sphere. He argues for an ontology of the political that acknowledges the constitutive conflict and plurality inherent in democratic societies. For Marchart politics is not merely a set of procedures for decision-making but a space of contention where different social forces struggle for hegemony. In the context of radical democracy, political difference underscores the need to recognise and embrace the irreducibility of political conflict. This perspective challenges the liberal democratic ideal of consensus and stable institutions, advocating instead for a more dynamic and agonistic view of democracy. By doing so, it moves the debate further away from liberal democracy and towards a more pluralistic and conflictual understanding of political life.

In the same vein, Helge Schwiertz's concept of 'democratic difference' (Schwiertz, 2021) extends the critique of liberal democracy by emphasising the diverse and often conflicting ways in which democracy can be practised and understood. Schwiertz argues that traditional models of citizenship and democratic participation are too restrictive and fail to account for the multiplicity of democratic experiences and aspirations. Thus, democratic difference highlights the importance of recognising and valuing these diverse democratic practices. It suggests that democracy should not be seen as a monolithic concept but rather as a field of contestation where different forms of participation and representation can coexist. This approach aligns with radical democracy's emphasis on inclusivity and the empowerment of marginalised voices, challenging the homogenising tendencies of liberal democratic frameworks. It also opens the possibility of rethinking novel democratic practices in social movements such as ecological citizenship or sustainable economies.

Schwiertz (2022) also introduces 'collective political subjectivation' to describe the process by which individuals and groups come together to form collective political identities. This concept emphasises the role of social movements and collective action in shaping political subjectivities and contesting dominant power structures. Thus, collective political subjectivation is central to radical democracy as it underscores the importance of collective agency and the creation of new political subjects. It highlights the potential for social movements to transform political landscapes and generate new forms of democratic participation and representation.

Engin Isin's discussion on various 'acts of citizenship' (Isin, 2008) shifts the focus from legal status and rights to the performative and agentic aspects of citizenship. By doing so, Isin expands the concept of citizenship beyond traditional state-centric notions and incorporates insights from the literature on acts of citizenship, citizenship beyond state sovereignty, and collective political subjectivation. Isin argues that citizenship is not just a legal designation but an active process of engagement and contestation. Thus, acts of citizenship are those moments when individuals or groups enact their rights and responsibilities, often in defiance of established norms and structures. Isin's insights are crucial to inform the political as well as theoretical potential of radical democracy as they highlight the capacity of ordinary people to challenge and reshape the political landscape. Put differently, by focusing on the performative dimension of citizenship, Isin's framework aligns with the radical democratic emphasis on active participation and the creation of new forms of political subjectivity.

Finally, Aoileann Ní Mhurchú (2014) explores the transnational and post-national dimensions of citizenship through expanding the concept of 'citizenship beyond state sovereignty'. For Ní Mhurchú traditional notions of citizenship tied to state sovereignty are increasingly inadequate in a globalised world where individuals and groups often operate across national boundaries. This perspective is valuable for radical democracy as it expands the scope of democratic engagement beyond the confines of the nation-state. It encourages the exploration of new forms of political community and solidarity that transcend state borders, thereby challenging the limitations of liberal democratic citizenship.

All in all, incorporating the concepts of political difference, democratic difference, collective political subjectivation, acts of citizenship, and citizenship beyond state sovereignty into the debate on radical democracy bestows on the latter the capacity to develop a richer and more comprehensive framework for understanding novel forms democratic engagement emerging from contemporary social movements, especially from those in non-European contexts. By embracing the inherent conflict and plurality within political life, recognising the diverse ways in which democracy can be practised, and expanding the notion of citizenship beyond traditional state-centric models, radical democracy has the potential to offer a more dynamic and empowering vision of democratic engagement.

To demonstrate this potential we now turn to two such movements from the Global South and discuss how novel forms of activism can guide and inspire the way radical democracy can be re-imagined and practised to meet the diverse, yet parallel, expectations of different peoples around the world.

## 3 Environmental Citizenship in Colombia

In the previous section, we argued that radical democracy fails to recognise how contemporary social movements entertain new expressions of citizenship through creative forms of activism. We also emphasised that the theory can be unable to interpret the actual experiences of contemporary social movements beyond a conventional interpretation of political citizenship (defined by rights and representation), thereby limiting the ability of radical democracy in formulating frameworks that can appreciate the 'rehearsals' of new social contracts envisioned by these social movements.

For us, new developments concerning radical democracy scholarship need to reconsider novel concepts and dimensions of citizenship from a broader perspective. Without a doubt, there is a need to analyse novel epistemologies that are emerging from social movements' prefigurative activism and other forms of collective political practice that are reconfiguring the dimensions of citizenship and political subjectivity with the aim of reimagining new social contracts.

To explore these issues and gain insights from a particular case study, this section will focus on how environmental social movements are exercising new dimensions of ecological citizenship in Colombia. The study will showcase the trajectory of environmental activism in recent decades and how this type of activism is shaping new expressions of ecological citizenship, aiming to invite a rethinking of social contracts between humanity and the environment from a posthumanistic perspective. We believe that Colombian environmental social movements provide useful insights to connect crucial ecological concerns with future notions of radical democracy. In other words, the case of Colombian environmental movements shows how it is possible to go beyond normative notions of citizenship (such as political citizenship) to frame environmental responsibilities as a key aspect of novel social contracts between humans and the planet.

## 3.1 Unpacking New Ecological Social Movements and Environmental Activism

Starting in the 1960s, the first wave of ecological social movements was self-consciously activist and unconventional, involving direct-protest collective actions designed to obstruct and draw attention to environmentally harmful policies and projects. During this early phase, various strategies were employed, including public education and media campaigns, community-driven initiatives, and traditional lobbying of policymakers and political figures. Raising awareness about ecological concerns involved practices like recycling, promoting green consumerism, and creating alternative communities, such as self-sustaining farms, worker cooperatives, and cooperative housing projects (Elliott & Esty, 2023; Lyon, 2020).

During that decade and until the end of the 1980s, ecological social movements exercised political actions focusing on electoral strategies, including the nomination of environmental candidates and the registration of green political parties. The rationale behind these actions was to try to exercise their political agency through the electoral system with the aim of changing things by following the rules of liberal democracy. Therefore, these environmentally conscious political parties were envisaged as a new type of political organisation that would bring the influence of the grassroots ecological movement directly to bear on the institutions of government, make environment a central concern of public policy, and render the state more democratic, transparent and accountable (Elliott & Esty, 2023; Sutton, 2019). Discussions about how to structurally change the economic model were not necessarily at the centre of these political dynamics.

In retrospect, we can easily argue that some ecological social movements at the time (particularly those in the United Kingdom, the United States, Germany,

Belgium, and Australia) put so much faith in the value and effectiveness of electoral politics. In other words, the exercise of political citizenship through participation in the electoral process was the main effort for these social movements to increase the public's awareness regarding environmental issues, encouraging traditional political parties to address ecological concerns. As such, the approach is in line with the orthodoxy of radical democratic theory, which privileges the political dimension of citizenship to catalyse social change, without reflecting that the compromises necessary for electoral success invariably undermine the ethos of grassroots democracy, the value of direct individual and collective action, and the capacity of agency of other crucial dimensions of citizenship.

However, since the beginning of the 1990s, ecological social movements and environmental activism have evolved significantly in both conceptual and practical terms. The work of Andrew Dobson (2004) was crucial to start rethinking the relationship between citizenship and the environment. Dobson argued that ecological citizenship cannot be fully articulated in terms of the two great traditions of citizenship (liberal and civic republican) with which we have been bequeathed. For this reason, Dobson developed an original theory of ecological citizenship that focuses on duties as well as rights, and these duties are owed non-reciprocally, by those individuals and communities who occupy unsustainable amounts of ecological space, to those who occupy too little. By addressing a post-cosmopolitan perspective, this work was a pioneer to discuss other dimensions of citizenship that can go beyond the political-centred focus.

From this perspective, ecological citizenship reconfigured the notion of political space as not localised in the state or in the municipality, or in the ideal speech community of cosmopolitanism, but in the ecological footprint that individuals and communities can generate. This approach contrasts with fiscal incentives and policy bills as a way of encouraging people to act more sustainably, in the belief that the former is more compatible with the long-term and deeper shifts of attitude and behaviour that sustainability requires. Thus, this notion of ecological citizenship is a valuable example of how to address other dimensions of citizenship (environmental dimension in this case) as a valid mechanism to consider novel concepts of radical democracy.

Here we identify five principal elements that shape the actions of contemporary ecological social movements and environmental activists that could be seen as different from previous decades in both conceptual and practical terms. The first element is how contemporary ecological social movements are embracing globalisation and transnational cooperation as a strategy to transcend national boundaries in order to address challenges such as climate change, biodiversity loss, and pollution on a global scale (Caniglia *et al.*, 2015). The second element is the making of climate change and global warming a central focus of the agenda for environmental activism. In previous decades, climate change was not as prominent an issue as it is today. Since the beginning of the new century, the scientific consensus on climate change and its potentially catastrophic effects has solidified. As a result, contemporary ecological social movements place a much stronger emphasis on addressing climate change and global warming, pushing for climate action, advocating for policy changes to mitigate its impacts, and developing disrupting direct actions to create public awareness (Stammen & Meissner, 2022).

The third element is related to how technological advancements and digital activism are changing the ways to do collective actions in both public and virtual spheres. Contemporary ecological social movements are embracing digital tools and social media networks to organise and mobilise communities more effectively. Online platforms have allowed for instant dissemination of information, coordination of campaigns and direct actions, producing engagement with a broader audience and making digital activism a significant driver of environmental change (Sutton, 2019). The fourth element is the recognition of intersectionality and inclusivity inside ecological social movements to interconnect environmental issues with other social justice concerns, including gender inequality, racial discrimination, and economic disparities (Goodman, 2017). The result of emphasising intersectionality and inclusivity has led to a more diverse and holistic approach to environmental and ecological activism in recent years.

The final element we recognise among the ecological movements is the rise in collective and direct actions focusing on holding corporations accountable for their environmental practices and advocating for responsible consumerism. Strategies and calls for sustainable business practices, corporate transparency, and eco-friendly products have become central to the work of contemporary ecological social movements (Stammen & Meissner, 2022). This element in combination with the rise of youth-led environmental movements (e.g., Fridays for Future or School Strike 4 Climate) provides ecological and environmental issues more prominence in mainstream politics and public discourse, with the hope of holding political leaders accountable for their environmental policies.

It is clear that as a result of the actions and elements of these new ecological social movements and environmental activism, we are witnessing the transformation of Dobson's initial conceptualisation of ecological citizenship towards a more holistic approach into the concept of environmental citizenship (Hadjichambis & Reis, 2020). This novel perspective of environmental citizenship is defined as the responsible pro-environmental behaviour of citizens who act as agents of change in the private and public sphere, on a local, national, and global scale, through individual and collective actions, in the direction of solving contemporary environmental problems, preventing the creation of new environmental concerns, achieving sustainability as well as developing a healthy relationship with nature (Hadjichambis & Reis, 2020).

Furthermore, this framework of environmental citizenship includes the practice of environmental rights and duties, as well as the identification of the underlying structural causes of ecological degradation. It is also stressing the main environmental problems and the development of the willingness and the competencies for critical and active engagement, and civic participation, to address those structural causes in order to act individually and collectively, taking into account inter- and intra-generational justice. Thus, this new framework offered by environmental citizenship can give us important tools to readdress the relationship between radical democracy and ecological concerns from a more holistic perspective.

## 3.2 Ecological Social Movements and Environmental Activism: Lessons from Colombia

Colombia is the second most biodiverse country in the world. As a matter of fact, per square kilometre, the country is the most biodiverse, hosting close to 10 per cent of the planet's biodiversity. There are more bird, amphibian, butterfly, and frog species in Colombia than anywhere else in the world (WWF, 2023). However, it is one of the deadliest countries in the world for human rights defenders, environmentalists, members of ecological social movements, and others defending land rights (Global Witness, 2012). In some parts of the country (particularly in the Amazon and the Orinoco River basin) being associated with any ecological or environmental social movement can be seen as a high-risk activity, suffering from high rates of criminalisation, physical violence, murder, kidnapping, internal displacement, and forced disappearance (Alzate, 2022; Scheidel *et al.*, 2020).

According to the international NGO Global Witness, more than 1,700 homicides of environmental activists were recorded globally over the past decade, an average of a killing nearly every two days, with Brazil, Colombia, the Philippines, Mexico, and Honduras being the deadliest countries (Global Witness, 2022). Just in 2022, Colombia was accounting for 186 killings, or 46 per cent, of the global total registered for the previous year (Front Line Defenders, 2023). Also last year, Colombia recorded the highest number of lethal attacks against members of ecological social movements, with eighty-eight environmental and indigenous rights defenders killed (47 per cent of the mentioned national total of 186).

In 2016 a peace agreement was put in place between the Colombian government and the former guerrilla group of the Revolutionary Armed Forces of Colombia (FARC), ending more than six decades of armed conflict in the country. A year after the signature of the peace agreement, armed gangs, paramilitary groups, and transnational illicit drug trafficking organisations started threatening and murdering community leaders, human rights defenders, and environmental activists who have been trying to protect Colombia's forest from destruction by mining, lumber, and oil companies in territories previously controlled by the FARC.

Following Llano-Arias (2014), Richardson & McNeish (2021), and Coombe & Jefferson (2021), we can identify six principal environmental issues in Colombia: deforestation, illegal mining, land rights and displacement, pollution, climate change vulnerability, and armed conflict dynamics. Without a doubt, deforestation is the main concern on this list. For example, deforestation in the Colombian Amazon has surged, surpassing 250,000 acres in three of the last four years. According to Murillo et al., rainforest sheltering spectacular biodiversity is being razed for cattle ranching and corporate farms, oil palm production, fossil fuel extraction, illegal gold mining and logging. Leaders of local communities and members of ecological social movements whose water is being poisoned and whose land has been devastated have provided the last line of defence against this ecological destruction (Murillo *et al.*, 2023). Thus, other natural habitats in the country have been threatened by deforestation through activities of agriculture expansion and illegal coca cultivation.

Nevertheless, since the 1970s, ecological social movements in Colombia have been crucial in enhancing awareness about environmental conflicts. It has also played a vital role in fostering opposition to megaprojects that have resulted in severe negative consequences for both communities and territories. According to Tarazona-Pedraza (2010) and Llano-Arias (2014), environmental activism in Colombia has been bringing together from the beginning multiple groups of individuals, grassroots organisations, and collectives who, from different perspectives, have dedicated their efforts to defending common goods, natural resources, and the quality of human life. By doing symbolic, cultural, and political actions, environmentalist movements in Colombia have opposed and mobilised against large-scale infrastructure projects that jeopardise natural and ecological reserves, in particular, water resources.

According to Tobasura-Acuña (2007), Colombia's environmental movement differs from the early defensive nature of the European environmental movement, which focused on issues such as nuclear energy and the arms race.

Instead, Colombia's movement is characterised as fluid, heterogeneous, and an ongoing social construct. It brings together a diverse range of rational and alternative perspectives, all aimed at discovering solutions for nature and environment preservation. Consequently, ecological social movements in Colombia are deeply intertwined with demands concerning class, race, inequality, and strategies to fight against poverty. This is particularly pronounced among peasants, campesinos, and rural communities in the country. Also, the pioneers of ecological activism in Colombia found inspiration in the outcomes of the first International United Nations Conference on the Human Environment in Stockholm in 1972, and in debates regarding the thesis presented the same year in the report The Limits to Growth by the Club of Rome about the relationship between growth and the environment.

In 1983, seventy distinct environmental movements and grassroots initiatives convened at the inaugural Ecological Organisations Conference (Econgente 83) in the city of Pereira. During this event, they collectively established the Colombian Environmental Movement as an umbrella organisation, known as MAC (Movimiento Ambiental Colombiano). The establishment of this new organisation resulted in two primary outcomes: first, a collective consensus regarding the interpretation of concepts such as ecology, the ecological movement, and development; and second, the establishment of a framework for coordinating collaborative collective sociopolitical actions on a national level. However, the most significant outcome was the formulation of the inaugural Colombian Ecological Manifesto, which delineated five key points: (1) The Earth serves as humanity's abode; allowing its destruction would culminate in our own demise, (2) The imperative lies not only in safeguarding our habitat, but also in protecting its inhabitants, (3) Societies rooted in consumption and wastefulness not only tarnish their own domains but also jeopardise others' well-being, (4) Predatory states not only deplete our resources but also impose technologies that frequently ravage our ecosystems, and (5) Within predatory states, individuals and institutions often endorse the relinquishment of our resources and the degradation of our environment (Guerrero, 2010).

Due to nationwide grassroots environmental activism and the strategic development of collective actions across the country, the Political Constitution of Colombia of 1991 is referred to in the country as the 'green constitution' or 'ecological constitution' (Melo, 2018). This constitution recognises the fundamental right to a healthy environment and was crafted in alignment with the primary international concerns surrounding environmental preservation and biodiversity during that era. Consequently, the constitution, in its principles, mandates, and obligations, is designed to achieve two main objectives: (i) the comprehensive safeguarding of the environment and (ii) the establishment of a sustainable development model. Two years following the constitution's enactment, and subsequent to heightened pressure from environmental groups, the Colombian government passed Law 99. This law provided a definition for sustainable development as follows: 'That which leads to economic growth, an improved quality of life, and social well-being, all without depleting the renewable natural resource base that sustains it, and without causing harm to the environment or infringing upon the rights of future generations to use it in accordance with their own needs' (Law 99, Republic of Colombia, 1993). Hence, it can be asserted that Colombia's constitution deems environmental protection not only as a right but also as an indispensable prerequisite for the survival of both communities and territories (Melo, 2018).

Nevertheless, the primary lessons derived from the Colombian Environmental Movement do not stem from its ability to shape public policies or sway political consensus. Instead, the most significant insights have emerged from the manner in which they exercise other dimensions of environmental citizenship towards environmental democratisation during the armed conflict and in post-war Colombia. This involvement notably encompassed the safeguarding primary of water resources, the implementation of collective actions to bring awareness to the link between ecological damage by extractive companies and its impact on the pursuit of truth and justice for the victims of the armed conflict, and the development of posthumanist approaches for integrating indigenous knowledge into contemporary environmental activism.

According to Roa (2016) and Ramírez (2023), the collective actions of social movements for environmental democratisation began in Colombia in 2004 in response to the exponential expansion of extractive activities and socio-environmental conflicts driven by armed conflict, legal and illegal transnational actors, and governmental policies aimed at transforming Colombia into a mining country. Since the beginning of the new century, one of the main objectives of the Colombian Environmental Movement has been to foster different sociocultural collective actions to protect water sources, safeguard local sustainable economies, create awareness regarding the link between ecological damage and the impact of the armed conflict in rural regions of the country, and the development of alternative visions to halt extractivism. Thus, the experience of one particular organisation inside the Colombian Environmental Movement, the Living Rivers Movement (Movimiento Ríos Vivos) in the County of Antioquia, is crucial to understanding the relevance of exercising other dimensions of environmental citizenship from a posthumanistic approach to the case of Colombia.

## 3.3 Environmental Citizenship and the Living Rivers Movement

The Living Rivers Movement is an umbrella organisation comprising fifteen grassroots environmental initiatives established in 2008 with the aim of halting the construction of the Hidroituango Dam on the Cauca River, near the municipality of Ituango in Northern Antioquia. Currently under construction by the Public Enterprises of Medellin (Empresa Públicas de Medellin, EPM), the Hidroituango Dam impacts more than 26,000 hectares and 27 municipalities. Upon completion of the project, approximately 4,500 hectares of land will be submerged. The Living Rivers Movement asserts that EPM bears responsibility for floods, landslides, deforestation, pollution, mass fish deaths, illegal logging, and improper disposal of wood and trash resulting from the dam's construction. These impacts have been disregarded by EPM in relation to the environmental significance and importance of the Cauca River, the second most important river in Colombia, in the livelihoods, culture, and economy of the local communities (Front Line Defenders, 2019).

The Hidroituango Dam's negative ecological impacts, as outlined in the Environmental Impact Assessment (EIA) made by EPM (2007), encompass a wide range of environmental, social, and economic concerns. These include air pollution, surface and groundwater pollution, changes in the quality of reservoir water, alterations in the fluvial dynamics of the Cauca River, modification of soil physical and chemical properties, landscape modification, changes in vegetation cover, habitat loss or fragmentation, death and displacement of fauna species, increased pressure on natural resources, alterations in fish community species abundance within the Cauca River basin, changes in biotope and benthic community structures, proliferation of disease vectors, the transformation from lotic to lentic environments, effects on identified archaeological sites, transformation of cultural systems among affected populations, involuntary forced population displacement and disruption of living conditions, an influx of foreign populations, increased demand for public and social services, and alteration of the regional economy (EPM, 2007).

Furthermore, Antioquia is the Colombian county with the highest number of victims from the former Colombian armed conflict, totalling 1.4 million, and it was the region where 20 per cent of all the violence during the armed conflict occurred, with 2,261,383 violent incidents over 50 years of war (Comision de la Verdad, 2022). There are four main reasons why the conflict was particularly intense in this region, and environmental activists were among the primary victims. First, nearly 70 per cent of Colombia's energy resources are concentrated in this area, making it also a strategically significant corridor within the armed conflict. Environmental activists also played an active role in holding energy companies accountable. Second, within the logic of the Colombian armed conflict, environmental activists became both war booty and specific targets for combatants. Given the strong patriarchal nature of the society in this region, targeting environmental activists proved to be a potent strategy for weakening local communities and disrupting their family structures. Third, the targeting of civilians as a method of warfare was a characteristic feature. This strategy was employed by both illegal and legal armed groups and became a central objective of military operations. Killing environmental activists allowed them to demonstrate power, assert superiority, lay claim to particular territories against rivals, and erode the social support base of opposing armed groups. A final explanation rests in the construction of a regime of terror in the region, where guerrilla and paramilitary groups utilised extreme cruelty to dehumanise their adversaries in war (Tamayo Gomez, 2012, 2022).

The former armed conflict situation in Antioquia provides a comprehensive reference for understanding the dynamics of the war in Colombia. Antioquia stood as one of the initial regions where guerrilla groups employed landmines to gain territorial control over the Colombian army. It also became a breeding ground for the systematic implementation of massacres against civilians, a war strategy deployed by paramilitary squads to spread fear and terror throughout the country, subjecting the civilian population to enduring suffering (Estrada, 2010). Consequently, the citizens of Antioquia experienced the full spectrum of war-related consequences: stigmatisation, forced displacements, massacres, persecution, marginalisation, extrajudicial executions, and torture. They fell victim to a myriad of human rights violations and abuses (García de la Torre & Aramburo, 2011; Tamayo Gomez, 2017). This culminated in three main characteristics that defined Antioquia in the context of the Colombian armed conflict: first, the persistent clashes between different illegal and legal armed groups vying for territorial control and its natural resources; second, the co-optation of local institutions, including councils and local governments, by illicit forces to undermine local democracy and seize economic resources; and finally, the establishment of illicit economies centred around deforestation, drug trafficking, kidnapping, and extortion, significantly impacting both local and regional economies (NCHM, 2018; Tamayo Gomez, 2022; UNDP, 2010).

However, concerning the construction of the Hidroituango Dam, one of the most detrimental impacts of this hydroelectric project has been on Colombia's ongoing transitional justice process. The dam's construction led to the flooding of extensive rural areas in Antioquia, where mass graves containing unidentified bodies from the armed conflict had been buried. This has undermined future investigations and the pursuit of truth, justice, and reparation for the victims.

Also, this is an example in relation to how a high-impact civil engineering initiative in the midst of an armed conflict or in a post-war situation needs to be conscious of its effect on human security, peacebuilding efforts, and the implementation of transitional justice mechanisms.

One of the most devastating outcomes of the former Colombian armed conflict is the number of disappeared and missing people. According to the NCHM (2018), the International Committee of the Red Cross (2018), and Colombia's Truth and Reconciliation Commission (2022), there is an estimation that the armed conflict left 210,000 people missing from 1958 to 2018. To put this in perspective, this surpasses the number of missing people registered during the dictatorship years in the Southern Cone countries of Argentina, Chile, Paraguay, and Uruguay. The number of people missing in Colombia could fill six professional football pitches and occupy more than two times the capacity of Wembley Stadium in London. Of the missing, 87 per cent are civilians, and 13 per cent are former combatants (Comision de la Verdad, 2022; NCHM, 2018).

Without a doubt, the most critical humanitarian challenge currently facing Colombia during its transitional justice processes is the task of finding the people who have disappeared due to the conflict (Comision de la Verdad, 2022; Tamayo Gomez, 2022, 2023). According to the project Front Line Defenders (2019), the construction of the Hidroituango Dam has also resulted in the disappearance and forced displacement of hundreds of people in the region, along with the deaths of hundreds more. Many families are still searching for the human remains of their loved ones, and the flooding of hundreds of hectares of land has made further investigations of mass graves and the bodies interred there impossible. This severe limitation impedes efforts to achieve justice and prevent the recurrence of such atrocities.

In essence, the construction of the Hidroituango Dam by EPM is having severe ecological and humanitarian impacts. It is destroying the dry tropical forest surrounding the Cauca River, an already fragile ecosystem that is at risk of disappearing from the planet. Additionally, this action is aiding perpetrators of the Colombian armed conflict in evading accountability and responsibility. In 2016, The Living Rivers Movement reported that EPM was felling the forest, raising the risk of landslides, species migration, and the loss of nationally protected plant species. This situation further increases the risk of losing landmarks crucial for finding the bodies of missing individuals. Furthermore, fishing and farming communities are losing their livelihoods due to the Hidroituango Dam, while fish in the Cauca River are dying, and displaced communities are unable to cultivate food on their lands anymore. In short, the impact of this project on the region's inhabitants has been devastating.

In this context, since 2009, alongside the organisation of public demonstrations, rallies, meetings, and other conventional forms of direct and collective action, the Living Rivers Movement has been engaged in the implementation of three distinct types of collective actions, exercising another dimension of their environmental citizenship. The first is the initiative Cañoneros y cañoneras contra el olvido (Canyon women and Canyon men against oblivion), a project for groups of victims wanting to recover victims' collective memory and the significance and importance of nature in places where massacres of civilians happened or where the bodies of missing persons are presumed to be buried. By organising plays, pantomimes, and other artistic performances in the main square of the municipality of Ituango, the main aim of this collective action is to commemorate their victims and create awareness regarding the people who disappeared in Northern Antioquia during the armed conflict and how the war has affected the Cauca River. This initiative involves the recreation of catholic religious rituals associated with purgatory in order to help the souls of the missing to be ready for heaven (90 percent of the Colombian population adheres to Christianity).

Nevertheless, the most interesting aspect of this initiative lies in its posthuman perspective. The culminating activity of Cañoneros y cañoneras contra el olvido involves a nocturnal pilgrimage to the Cauca River. The Living Rivers Movement acknowledges, through their collective actions, that the world we live in is not human-centred. They argue that we live in a world where interlinked connections and relationships between humans, non-humans, and more-than-humans systems shaped our communal existence. By integrating indigenous knowledge from the local community, the Living Rivers Movement emphasises the significance of valuing all environmental interconnections and, in particular, water-human life relationships. During the river pilgrimage, participants join in singing chants that decry the Hidroituango Dam and perform nostalgic songs that reminisce about the harmonious community life that existed before the commencement of this hydroelectric project.

After arriving at the Cauca River at midnight, the participants began fishing using only their hands and a torch, re-enacting ancestral techniques. Throughout the fishing activity, all participants chanted the words: 'The Cauca River is dead, the Cauca River is dirty. The Cauca River used to provide us with everything. We are the river; we will save the river; we will heal the river' (NCHM, 2019). Once the communal fishing comes to an end, the participants light candles inside small wooden replicas of artisanal fishing boats. This marks the most solemn aspect of the activity. These small boats contain the names of individuals who are missing and presumed to be buried in the Cauca River. Before releasing the boat replicas into the river's current, one of the organisers addresses the audience, stating: 'I send this light for those comrades who have died in our struggle. May this be a beautiful memory that we offer to this river, which is no longer just a river but a part of all of us. This light is for all the loved ones whom the river has embraced and taken without our knowing about them. May they receive this small light with deep affection, and may they realise that they are not forgotten. With this light, I advocate for peace for everyone, even for those who have caused us great harm, because we all deserve to live' (NCHM, 2019). As more than 120 small wooden replicas carrying an equal number of candles are released, the event culminates with a minute of silence, a solemn tribute to both the river and the victims.

The second initiative is named 'Cuerpos Gramaticales' (Grammatical Bodies). This undertaking is a political-artistic performative action designed within the framework of Agroarte methodology. It seeks to narrate stories of violence inflicted upon bodies, nature, and the territory from a posthuman perspective. 'Cuerpos Gramaticales' engages in a sequence of activities prior to the collective action, involving the symbolic and material planting of bodies in public spaces to recreate the individuals buried in mass graves. The use of theatre performances, dance, poetry, and writing is integral to these activities. The Living Rivers Movement has conducted ten performative actions under the umbrella of 'Cuerpos Gramaticales' between 2014 and 2018, spanning across Ituango and Medellin, the capital of Antioquia County.

The framework of Agroarte spins around the posthuman metaphor of a tree deeply rooted in the defence of life, the environment, and all ecological manifestations. Its trunk symbolises the strength of survival amidst armed conflicts, presenting a collective action capable of fostering a process of victims' collective memory 'from below' (Tamayo Gomez, 2022). This framework also encompasses collective actions aimed at fostering 'the democratisation of pain' (a transformation of personal experiences of loss into shared public knowledge) as expressions of environmental citizenship (Tamayo Gomez, 2022). According to The Living Rivers Movement, the seed symbolically encapsulates the latency of the memory it carries, while the wind disperses it, giving rise to interconnected new native forests and embodying a profound metaphor of human and non-human entities.

As Cañoneros y cañoneras contra el olvido, 'Cuerpos Gramaticales' is a collective action that provokes reflections about truth, memory, and recognition. Participants who get involved in this action design the whole process and decide their own reasons for taking part in the planting: healing, protest, a symbol of planting new family roots after suffering internal displacement, connecting with the land, letting go, starting a new life or forgiveness, just to name a few. This collective action usually ends with a final public performance during which the project's participants collectively 'planting' themselves with flowers into the ground in a public place to create catharsis. As one of The Living Rivers Movement members expressed, the symbolic sowing of bodies represents the metaphor of life where, as soon as the seed grows, blossoms and produces fruits, it becomes part of the world's socio-environmental system. In her words 'it is about finding our roots, not just the ones in the deep and heartfelt earth, but also with our own roots, which lay within the immensity of every single person' (Alvarez, 2017).

The third collective action is a cross-media strategy named 'Saborcito Cañonero' (Canyon's Taste), which involves the creation of fanzines, poetry, comic stories, photographic exhibitions, the establishment of local community kitchens, and the production of audio-visual material. This strategy aims to showcase local cultural traditions and environmental cosmogonies related to food and cooking. Through this collective effort, online videos are created to present recipes highlighting Antioquia's local cuisine, accompanied by narratives about local history, stories of resistance by members of The Living Rivers Movement, and accounts detailing the connections between humans, non-humans, and nature. Thus, it is a strategy that addresses the relationship between the material and the symbolic dimension of food and cooking.

Furthermore, this collective action involves the utilisation of medicinal herbs in cooking, emphasising the significance of local indigenous knowledge. This effort encompasses the collaborative development of catalogues featuring medicinal herbs, the creation of innovative recipes in which local herbs serve as primary ingredients, and the production of fanzines that convey narratives highlighting the importance of food and food security within local communities. Thus, comic stories showcase representations and narratives around how the Cauca River used to provide all ingredients for a healthy diet around the consumption of fish, and by what means cooking is a connection between rural work, everyday activities, and the river as a central part of communal life.

However, one of the relevant and important aspects of this initiative is how the Living Rivers Movement promotes cooking as an excuse to start open and difficult conversations. Questions, including 'What was the last meal you had the day before you were displaced from your land by war?, 'What was the last dinner you cooked in the river on the day you were displaced by the Hidroituango Dam?', 'What was the last cooking ingredient you used when you saw your brother for the last time?' or 'What was the last meal your mother or grandmother made before she was killed?' are distributed in small fanzines to catalyse questions during cooking activities at the local community kitchens in order to reflect on the past.

As Smart (1994) and Domaneschi (2019) argued, worlds of food and cooking are often suitable metaphors for understanding vital aspects of communal sociocultural life. Also, the collective action 'Saborcito Cañonero' is stressing the idea of cooking and food as social spaces (Poulain, 2005), highlighting how food production, food consumption, and the practice of cooking are structural dimensions of the social organisation of human groups. From a posthuman perspective, this initiative is addressing an intersection between human and non-human elements, reimagining the reciprocal position assumed by human action, in this case, cooking, and materiality (e.g., cooking ingredients, local herbs), and the consequent valorisation attributed to the two dimensions in different contexts created by 'Saborcito Cañonero'.

Moreover, these three initiatives (Cañoneros y cañoneras contra el olvido, Cuerpos Gramaticales, and Saborcito Cañonero) are grassroots collective actions highlighting the relevance and cruciality of exercising other dimensions of environmental citizenship from a posthuman approach. An important lesson from those experiences concerning novel epistemologies that are emerging from social movements' prefigurative activism, that are reconfiguring the dimensions of citizenship practice and political subjectivity with the aim of reimagining new social contracts, is the way that The Living Rivers Movement is addressing concepts including recognition, social justice 'from below', solidarity, and memory to be recognised as main environmental actors based on their particular sociocultural identities.

It is clear in this case that this environmental movement does not only aspire for recognition as a rational actor who represents singular sociopolitical identities in the public sphere (traditional political approach to the construction of normative social contracts). It also claims a more robust set of rights (in our case, environmental rights) in order to exercise other dimensions of their citizenship during transitional justice processes, the struggles against EPM, finding ways to reconcile posthumanism with human liberal values, and addressing the intersection between gender justice, indigenous rights, ecological memory, racial justice, and interrelations of sexuality and identity.

In other words, the case of the Living Rivers Movement is relevant for comprehending how collective actions and grassroots initiatives can go beyond narrow institutional focus and normative prescriptions, challenging conventional conceptualisation of the full range of roles social movements can play in shaping democracy. It is to recognise environmental citizenship as a dynamic, diverse, and contextual process where actions of social solidarity, memory, and recognition are providing means of expression for victims and survivors that are not open to them through the formal discourse of citizenship. Furthermore, there is an absence of understanding of what means social movements can exercise their agency to explore novel and unofficial social justice mechanisms of reparation and recognition in post-conflict scenarios.

The principal challenge is how to promote environmental citizenship initiatives of social solidarity, memory, and recognition that might help local communities to comprehend contested sociopolitical ideas, contest official versions of the past, support inclusive processes of social justice, and create new social contracts. This would improve our understanding of how the development of environmental citizenship actions can be a powerful mechanism for claiming truth, justice, and reparation in contested societies. Comprehending new dimensions of environmental citizenship as a crucial aspect to create novel social contracts stresses the importance of recognising social movements' agency in supporting inclusive sociocultural processes beyond official agendas and narratives, appreciating environmental movements as subjects with their own agency, projects, priorities, and organisational ability.

It is safe to argue, then, that by moving away from the conventional definitions of citizenship as strictly in political terms, the environmental movement in Colombia firmly recognises and engages with crucial intersections between social justice and rights. It acknowledges that true ecological awareness necessitates comprehensive consideration of gender justice, indigenous rights, ecological memory, racial justice, and the complex interrelations of sexuality and identity. Understanding and addressing these interconnections are pivotal to creating a sustainable and equitable future for all. Thus, gender justice serves as a cornerstone of the environmental movement in Colombia. Recognising that gender equality is inherently linked to environmental well-being, the movement advocates for equal access to resources, participation, and decision-making for all genders (Bell, 2016). It acknowledges that diverse voices and experiences are essential to forge the path towards a more sustainable and inclusive society. Also, indigenous rights are deeply intertwined with environmental stewardship. Indigenous communities in Colombia have sustained harmonious relationships with nature for centuries, instilling a profound understanding of ecological balance and the importance of land preservation (Mazzocchi, 2020). The environmental movement honours and supports the rights of indigenous peoples, respecting their knowledge, traditions, and connection with their ancestral lands.

Furthermore, ecological memory acknowledges the importance of learning from the past to forge a sustainable future. Recognising the wisdom held by diverse cultures and their ancestral knowledge, the Colombian environmental movement seeks to preserve and incorporate traditional ecological knowledge into modern conservation efforts (Nykvist & von Heland, 2014). By acknowledging and respecting ecological memory, we can learn from ancient practices and avoid repeating past mistakes. In this context, racial justice is a fundamental aspect of environmentalism. The environmental movement acknowledges that marginalised communities often bear the brunt of environmental degradation and climate change impacts due to systemic racism and environmental injustice.

By addressing racial disparities, the environmental movement aims to rectify the disproportionate burden faced by these communities and create equitable solutions that benefit all (Alvarez, 2023).

Finally, the environmental movement recognises and values the interrelations of sexuality and identity within the broader ecological discourse. Understanding that LGBTQIA+ individuals face unique environmental challenges, the movement advocates for LGBTQIA+ rights and inclusion. It promotes an inclusive approach that embraces diverse identities and ensures that environmental spaces are safe and welcoming for all individuals. In sum, the environmental movement in Colombia takes a holistic approach, recognising the intricate web of connections between various social justice issues. It emphasises gender justice, indigenous rights, ecological memory, racial justice, and the interrelations of sexuality and identity as critical factors in fostering a sustainable, inclusive, and equitable future for our planet and all its inhabitants.

## 3.4 Environmental Citizenship and Radical Democracy in Colombia

As we have demonstrated above, the environmental and ecological movement in Colombia is highly relevant to a more sophisticated theoretical framework for radical democracy. This relevance can be articulated through six key aspects that highlight the transformative potential of these movements in fostering inclusive, participatory, and equitable radical democratic practices.

The first aspect is *grassroots mobilisation and participatory democracy*. The environmental and ecological movement in Colombia, and in particular The Living Rivers Movement, have been characterised by robust grassroots mobilisation. These movements often emerge from local communities directly affected by environmental degradation and resource extraction. Local communities in Colombia have organised to protect their territories from mining, deforestation, and other destructive activities. These initiatives exemplify participatory democracy, where decision-making power is decentralised and vested in the hands of those most impacted by environmental issues. Such grassroots mobilisation encourages active citizen participation and enhances democratic engagement at the local level. Thus, many Indigenous and Afro-Colombian communities have established autonomous governance structures to manage their natural resources. These self-governance practices challenge the top-down approach of the state and demonstrate the potential for more localised and participatory forms of democracy.

The second aspect is the *intersection of environmental and social justice*. The Colombian environmental movement is deeply intertwined with issues of social justice, making it a powerful advocate for a more inclusive and equitable form of democracy. Environmental degradation in Colombia often disproportionately affects marginalised communities, including Indigenous peoples, Afro-Colombians, and rural peasants. The environmental movement highlights these injustices and advocates for policies that address both ecological and social inequalities. This intersectional approach ensures that the voices of marginalised communities are included in democratic processes. Also, Colombia has a high number of environmental defenders who risk their lives to protect their territories. The movement for their protection and recognition underscores the need for a democracy that safeguards the rights of those who stand up against powerful economic interests.

The third aspect is how the ecological movement in Colombia is *reimagining citizenship and collective responsibility*. Environmental movements in Colombia promote a broader and more inclusive concept of citizenship that goes beyond traditional liberal democratic notions. For example, the movement advocates for ecological citizenship where individuals and communities see themselves as stewards of the environment. This expanded notion of citizenship includes responsibilities towards the environment and future generations, fostering a collective sense of duty and care for natural resources. At the same time, many Colombian communities engage in commoning practices, managing shared resources collectively. These practices challenge the neoliberal focus on private property and individual ownership, promoting a communal approach to resource management. Such practices enhance social cohesion and community resilience, key components of a robust democracy.

The fourth aspect is how this movement is *enhancing democratic participation through environmental advocacy*. Environmental advocacy in Colombia has led to the development of new forms of democratic participation and governance, as the case of *Living Rivers* is showing us. Environmental movements often organise assemblies and forums to discuss and address environmental issues. These gatherings provide a platform for inclusive dialogue and collective decision-making, empowering communities to have a direct say in matters that affect their lives. Moreover, the environmental movement in Colombia has also spurred legal innovations, such as the recognition of the rights of nature from a posthumanistic approach. For instance, granting the Atrato River legal personhood was a groundbreaking development that reflects a shift towards a more holistic and inclusive legal framework. Such legal recognition can be seen as a step towards a more radical and transformative form of democracy that acknowledges the intrinsic value of natural entities.

The fifth aspect is related to *fostering resilience and adaptive capacity*. The environmental movement in Colombia contributes to building resilient communities capable of adapting to environmental and social changes. By advocating for sustainable practices and protecting ecosystems, the environmental movement helps communities build resilience against climate change and other environmental threats. Resilient communities are better equipped to participate in and sustain democratic practices. The movement promotes adaptive governance models that are flexible and responsive to changing environmental conditions. This adaptability is crucial for fostering a dynamic and responsive democracy that can address contemporary challenges effectively.

The final aspect concerns *influencing national and global environmental policies*. Colombian environmental movements have also impacted national and international policy, demonstrating the potential for local activism to influence broader democratic frameworks. Thus, environmental activists in Colombia have successfully advocated for stronger environmental protections and policies at the national level. These policy changes reflect the power of collective action and participatory advocacy in shaping government actions and priorities (e.g., The Escazú Agreement).

All in all, the Colombian environmental movement is a part of global networks advocating for environmental justice and sustainability. This global solidarity reinforces the interconnectedness of local and global struggles and highlights the role of transnational activism in advancing democratic principles worldwide. Thus, the environmental and ecological movement in Colombia provides a compelling case for rethinking and revitalising radical democratic frameworks while it challenges the limitations of traditional liberal democratic models and offers innovative pathways for addressing the complex socio-environmental challenges. By emphasising grassroots participation, social and environmental justice, expanded notions of citizenship, and resilience, the case of The Living Rivers Movement demonstrates how radical democracy can be more inclusive, participatory, and equitable.

## 4 Building the Common in Türkiye

In this section we are turning our attention to the ways through which contemporary social movements prefigured and implemented new economic models as 'rehearsals' for a truly radical social order imagined beyond those offered by neoliberal capitalism or state socialism. Our aim is to flesh out our second claim regarding the 'blind spots' within the theory of radical democracy, i.e., how novel political practices that emerged from these movements surpassed the imagination of the radical democratic paradigm in building an alternative economic model. In order to demonstrate this, we focus on commoning practices and solidarity economies as they took root in Türkiye before, during, and after Gezi Park protests in 2013. Tracing the actual experience of radical democracy as it took root in Türkiye will help us understand how these practices shaped the political imagination of the activists towards building a future not confined to the binary of 'capitalism or socialism'.

## 4.1 Radical Democracy in Gezi Park

When the AKP government and its leader Recep T. Erdoğan laid their eyes on a small promenade at the heart of Istanbul to open it up for the construction of a shopping mall and a high-end residential complex, they were probably not expecting the reaction that became one of the biggest protests in modern Turkish history. The attempt to demolish Gezi Park had not caught public's attention except for a handful of environmental activists until the police began to violently handle the protest on the last days of May 2013. Powerful images of protestors being tear-gassed and battered spread rapidly through social media, igniting further riots across the city and the entire country. Following the retreat of the police after relentless clashes, a two-week occupation of the park began with a long list of diverse occupants, including urban grassroots organisations and neighbourhood associations; socialist political parties, radical left groups and platforms, environmentalists (such as those who were resisting against the third bridge on Bosporus), soccer fans of the prominent Istanbul clubs, and various small and big groups who identified as Kemalist nationalist, LGBTQIA+, feminist, anarchist and more. Looked closely, this colourful crowd comprised employees in precarious service-sector jobs; members of trade unions, chambers and associations (although they were not there to officially represent their organisations); university and high school students; white-collar professionals such as academics, journalists, doctors, lawyers, architects, and city planners; anti-capitalist Muslims; several deputies of the parliament; and politically non-affiliated citizens (Ercan Bilgiç & Kafkaslı, 2013; Kibar & Tatari, 2013; Konda, 2014; Uluğ & Acar, 2014).

This astonishing diversity was heralding the birth of something fundamentally new and radical in Turkish politics and society. Similar to the other square movements and occupations that stretched from Latin America and Europe to the Middle East and East Asia during the 2010s, novel radical democratic practices were at the centre of contentious politics during the Gezi movement, too. In the span of just a couple of years following the rise and demise of the occupation of Gezi Park, different forms of political activism (street fights, park forums, squat house anarchism, or simply meeting in a building) became part of a connected process of radical democratic mobilisation in Istanbul and across the country.

Indeed, a new modality of social existence emerged with the occupation: concerts and other recreational activities such as yoga, chess or soccer, movie screenings, activities for children as well as informative workshops on a variety of topics became commonplace (Mashallah Team, 2013). A library and a makeshift clinic were established immediately after the park was occupied. Meanwhile, donations including food, toiletries, and other needs were piling up as food stations started distributing food free of charge. Crews of volunteers worked in shifts to keep the park clean. All the while, barricades surrounded the park, and activists (both men and women, some of whom would be as young as sixteen) took turns as 'guards' while others were providing them with food and other needs (Atayurt, 2013: 27–28). There was also a media centre that served as the official press of the park commune. Humour remained strong in graffities, banners, slogans, satirical songs, and even by inventing a term 'chapulling' with which activists (and their collaborators in different corners of the world) re-appropriated the term *çapulcu (looter, maraudeur)* gifted to them by Erdoğan himself.

More importantly, the park became a lively space for interaction, communication, and political debate as an integral part of ongoing activism. Crowded assemblies could go on until midnight where participants followed special communication rules, showing respect for each other's sometimes hard-to-swallow opinions (Kibar & Tatari, 2013: 62–67). Early interviews with activists and observations by journalists revealed that themes such as diversity, tolerance, peaceful coexistence, community, freedom, and building a common future would often be raised in these forum meetings in the park (Güven, 2013). This would continue even after Gezi Park was dispersed by the police and when activists retreated to other public parks in the city and all around the country, holding public forums with hundreds of people attending to discuss the future of their rebellion. Numerous forums that emerged during this period created a vital sphere for the exercise of a novel type of political engagement that reflected the will of the emerging political community. Soon enough, they created their own communication protocols at the meetings where rotating speakers could voice their thoughts in the time allocated for them. Debates sometimes lasted for hours and involved pragmatic matters regarding the actions to be taken, but also broader political questions. As forum gatherings became more routine, they began to establish thematic sub-committees, some of which organised workshops and study-groups on themes such as women, children, arts, learning a new language, and so forth. With their radical democratic practices (with regard to participation, decision-making, division of labour, and mobilisation), and their deep distrust towards existing representative mechanisms, these forums became bedrocks for an alternative political existence and the creation of new political subjectivities.

One important characteristic of the forums was that activists utilised truly radical ways to arrive at collective decisions. They developed new habits and new roles, new rhythms which characterised new forms of life in common. Indeed, the horizontal organisational structure of park forums served as a fundamental characteristic of a new political experience defined by consensus-based decision-making, non-hierarchical, leaderless organisation, and so on, which could be defined as building 'the common'. Squat houses, community gardens and other local initiatives, too, were instances of crafting new spaces of solidarity and communication where constituting a new community around the common became the method of achieving justice and equality through radical democracy.

The radical democratic vision that centred around the defence of the commons in Türkiye did not begin with the Gezi uprising but dates back to the 1960s and 1970s (Fırat, 2018). But before we provide a critical overview of the struggles for fighting for the commons as an alternative, anti-capitalist form of social existence in the Turkish context, a brief discussion on the idea of the commons and commoning is in order.

## 4.2 From Defending the Commons to (Re)building the Common

Commons can be defined as a system 'in which resources are shared by a community of users/producers, who also define the modes of use and production, distribution and circulation of these resources through democratic and horizontal forms of governance' (De Angelis & Harvie, 2013: 280). Historically, commons were utilised to protect the community 'from the excesses of capitalist processes, and at times even allow them to avoid the discipline of capital' (Genç, 2018: 83). In more contemporary times, defending the commons became an important feature of the emancipatory struggles in the Global South for the survival of local communities through access to and sustainable use of natural resources as well as collective production. Yet it is the act of 'commoning' that turns commons into praxis rather than a mere reservoir of shared resources. In the mid-1990s and early 2000s, as the face of the anti-globalisation struggle, the Zapatista movement in Mexico was implementing various practices of commoning. Their methods inspired landless peasants' movements in different parts of the Global South, such as Brazil, Bolivia, and India, among others (Fırat, 2018: 69).

Hardly confined to rural mobilisation, commoning also became a method of struggle against the enclosure and privatisation of public spaces through gentrification and urban renewal projects. As such it became an act of self-defence against the neoliberal assault on the city and the social fabric it nurtures. Indeed, various movements of the poor and the precariat, such as occupying streets and roads against highway constructions, or the rise of squatting and other autonomous governance practices in certain cities in Europe, or factory occupations of Argentina in the early 2000s, or the rise of collective gardens and production cooperatives were all a part of this 'commoning' wave (Fırat, 2018: 69–70). It was with these social movements that commoning began to emerge as 'discursive and material practices that not only counter[ed] forces of enclosure but that also produce[d] a sense of place and community' in the urban context (Fırat, 2022: 1031).

It is important to think about commoning in relation with the broader idea of 'solidarity economy' which has become the conceptual and practical foundation of an alternative, non-capitalist economic model in the last decades (there is a growing literature on solidarity economy: Aykaç, 2017; Kawano *et al.*, 2010; Laville, 2023; North & Cato, 2017; Roelvink *et al.*, 2015; Speth & Courrier, 2020; Utting, 2015; Zitcer, 2021). Solidarity economy emerged and grew as a global movement to transform and transcend the capitalist economy to create a more just and sustainable alternative, as well as creating a network of national and regional initiatives around the same purpose. It gained prominence following the 2008 financial crisis but especially due to the looming ecological crisis. At its core, solidarity economy is an effort to imagine and implement economic alternatives in the face of the failures of neoliberal capitalism but also of state socialism and other state-dominated authoritarian systems (Kawano, 2020: 285). It seeks to develop a novel approach to economy along radical democratic lines and around the principles of solidarity, cooperation, mutualism, equity (in race, ethnicity, nationality, class, gender and other dimensions), participatory democracy, sustainability, and pluralism (Kawano, 2020: 286).

One of the key aspects of solidarity economies is that they imagine an economic system which is 'embedded in natural and social ecosystems' and as such does not shy away from attempting to transform the state as well to accommodate a broad range of socially and naturally sustainable practices (Kawano, 2020: 286). Food cooperatives, community land trusts, non-profit non-bank financial institutions, worker-owned factory production, community gardens, non-monetised exchange bazaars, care networks, and different forms of mutual aid disaster relief are all considered as expressions of non-capitalist alternatives under the umbrella of solidarity economy. Being more comprehensive than 'social economy' which adheres to the 'principles of democratic control by membership, solidarity, primacy of social and member interests over capital, and sustainability', solidarity economy emphasises systemic change that advocates the transformation of the state more along *autonomista* and anarchist principles, albeit not being limited to these (Kawano, 2020: 292–293). As Aykaç argues, 'although the idea and the principles of the solidarity economy are revolutionary, the strategy or the course of action toward the aforementioned objective is more transformative than it is revolutionary' (Aykaç, 2017: 11).

The major implication for contemporary social movements of the rise of solidarity economy, along with commoning as its main tool and driver, is the reversal in the temporal order of radical social change. In other words, instead of waiting for the transformation of institutions by force of a political revolution, practices of everyday life, regardless of where they were undertaken (in an encampment in an occupied park or square, or in a squat house, or even at regular forum meetings), became the revolution itself. Commoning as a form of political mobilisation in these movements rejected the state and market logic/power as the sole alternatives to organising principles of the existing social order. It offered a deeper critique with an alternative social organisation model in mind: a political project that attempts to restore a reworked form of solidarity that has been destroyed by neoliberalism when people lost their employment, residence, health, education and social bonds that held them together as a community. Therefore, contemporary social movements became a dual politics in which radical democracy simultaneously meant politics of mobilising (to protect and reclaim common resources) and politics of organising (to constitute a new community) against the neoliberal logic of social (dis)organisation. In this political context, the common served 'as both the form and the content of social relations that transcend the limitations and the market worshipping cynicism of contemporary capitalism' (Stavrides, 2020).

During the anti-austerity and pro-democracy movements of the 2010s, commoning became both a survival mechanism for the disadvantaged and marginalised, and a reaction by the urban middle class who experienced significant cultural and social impoverishment and loss of belonging due to the gentrification and transformation of their city. Although these movements emerged from their specific national contexts (such as in Brazil in 2013 when protestors took the streets to protest a hike in the price of public transportation) they were not 'insulated' cases but were in alliance with each other. They were globally connected also with respect to the methods they learnt from each other. In resisting the privatisation of common spaces and refusing dispossession, initiatives such as collective kitchens, healthcare centres, day-cares, non-commercial pharmacies, schools, producer cooperatives, exchange markets, and vegetable gardens, not to mention the open assemblies in park encampments and occupations, emerged as solidarist, collaborative, equalitarian, self-ruling, and radically democratic institutions of the collective will. It is through these non-capitalist practices that commoning moved beyond a mere act of collectively producing, defending, reclaiming and reproducing the material needs of a community outside the realm of the market and the state. Commoning extended itself to the 'co-production of new systems of values, of producing what is of common value together' (De Angelis, 2010: 958) which meant the reviving and redefining of the community as a political tool in the struggle for an alternative world. As such, reclaiming the commons and acts of commoning became both the paradigm of social transformation and motor of establishing a new social order through anti-capitalist institutions, relations, practices, and values.

## 4.3 Early Practices of Commoning in Türkiye

The term *müşterekler* ('commons') began to gain prominence in the lexicon of Turkish political activism during the late 1990s and early 2000s. But according to Duru, the continuing (and increasing) relevance of the concept itself stems from several reasons, including: a significant portion of the country's land still being owned by the state due to the heritage of the manorial system and Ottoman land law; forests still occupying a significant territory of the country; and the ongoing process of urbanisation the adverse consequences of which became more visible and pronounced in the face of increasing commodification of the land as well as the rising importance of sectors such as energy, tourism and construction that bring the most damage and destruction onto nature (Duru, 2018: 16). Duru also contends that one can find strong iterations of the commons as early as the first years of the Republic, more specifically in the Village Law of 1924. The law included articles that emphasised 'male and female villagers who have the right to choose the village headman and council of elders', and that 'most of the village work is carried out through collective participation of all villagers', and that 'people who have the right to shared goods such as mosques, schools, pastures, highlands and coppices and who live in nucleated or dispersed settlement patterns with their vineyards, gardens, and farms are the constituents of a village' (Duru, 2013). This is why the term *müşterekler* has often been associated with protests that resisted the privatisation of 'common resources', especially in the rural parts of the country (Fırat, 2018: 67–68). Most notably, protests against the commodification of natural resources and their transfer to big construction and energy companies, which had not begun but doubtlessly intensified under the AKP's construction-led growth model during the first decade of the twenty-first century, sparked first serious discussions about the commons (Adaman *et al.*, 2016: 21).

Resisting environmental destruction, pollution, construction of power plants, or opening up of new mines became primary reasons for mobilisation in environmental movements in the past two decades (Hazar-Kalnoya, 2021). Radical discourse and practices of commoning could be observed during numerous protests that resisted, among other things, the appropriation of land, eviction of peasants from these enclosed areas, prevention of traditional or alternative methods of agricultural production (Adaman *et al.*, 2016: 18). Among these, disrupting construction sites by sit-ins, barricades, and occupations often accompanied direct clashes with private or state security forces. What united them was their collective resistance to some form of enclosure of what they saw as their commons. The political topography of this activism extended from reclaiming and defending land, forests, pastures, rivers, or sometimes the whole planet to defending the 'national riches' against the economic imperialism of multinational companies, such as the resistance against gold mining in Bergama during the 1990s and the construction of a hydroelectric power plants in in the Black Sea region of the country since the early 2000s (Çobanoğlu, 2014). As such they became a defence of ecological and social life against dispossession and privatisation of which they collectively owned and utilised.

With the intensification of neoliberal urbanisation under the AKP rule, the centre of political activism and sites of commoning began to shift from rural areas to urban spaces, especially to big cities such as Istanbul. One of the most prominent actors in this form of activism has been neighbourhood associations. They became especially active in Istanbul during the early years of the AKP rule to struggle against renewal, gentrification and transformation projects in their districts but also against 'mega projects' such as the construction of a new airport, the third bridge on the Bosporus, plans for a new canal connecting Black Sea to Marmara Sea, and maritime ports constructions along the Bosporus such as Galataport, Haydarpaşaport and Haliçport. These neighbourhood associations and other environmentalist groups often formed platforms and alliances to promote education, information-sharing, and consciousness-raising activism (Genç, 2018: 85–86). Their efforts were joined by others to defend historical sites and public spaces in cities, particularly in Istanbul, such as the historical movie theatre Emek in the Beyoğlu district at the heart of the city (Fırat, 2022). Campaigns led by urban planners, lawyers, artists, and academics sought to extend their efforts beyond legal battles and generated a counter-discourse that entertained ideas such as accessibility, public interest, and cultural heritage (Genç, 2018: 88).

In order to resist the transfer of public spaces into private hands, counter-narratives in press releases, public protests or other events framed such attempts as 'theft' to raise awareness and mobilise the public. Reinstituting collective practices such as organising film festivals, concerts or other events, turning the privatised space into a collectively owned and utilised space became the very acts of commoning against attempts of enclosure. Turning these spaces into common places of everyday life where concerned individuals volunteered for various tasks such as food preparation, cleaning, and others. Such acts turned the space into a special form of existence where, in sharp contrast to neoliberalism's emphasis on the commercial value of the urban space, a non-capitalist form of togetherness, a new political subjectivity is experienced (Fırat, 2022). Moreover a new form of solidarity and sociality could now be imagined and prefigured through these acts of commoning against the destruction of the social under neoliberalism.

## 4.4 Commoning (in) Gezi Park and Beyond

Gezi Park protests and radical practices in their aftermath should be considered as a part of – if not the most notable example in – this historical lineage in defending, reclaiming, and rebuilding the commons in Türkiye. It emerged as an act for protecting a collectively utilised resource, a public park, against the state-enforced enclosure disguised as an urban renewal project. The main motivation behind the Gezi protests was to halt this relentless attack on the residents' 'right to the city'. Yet the uprising went beyond a mere act of defence and morphed into collective practices of producing and reproducing the common along the principles of solidarity, autonomy, justice, and self-organisation. The provision of food, shelter, healthcare, education, recreational activities and workshops, public gardens, and the division of labour for the overall maintenance of Gezi Park (and later the park forums and squat houses) were all undertakings that inherently prefigured a collective future beyond the AKP's vision of Islamist neoliberal urbanism in Istanbul (Akbulut, 2016: 291–292). In Ertaş's words, Gezi was a 'situated experience of creating and protecting (with barricades) an urban commons where the logic of neoliberal enclosure of public spaces could be subverted, giving way to new forms of relationality among people and with the spaces they occupy' (Ertaş, 2023).

Over time, the whole movement began to evolve from protecting the commons to constituting the common, carrying with it new 'values and principles as freedom, equality, reciprocity, solidarity, trust, and self-governance in a space where the state and capital were excluded' (Genç, 2018: 92). Various enactments of commoning became a source of new subjectification that began to change the lives of those who took part in this collective effort (Yazıcı & Fırat, 2013). The transformative power of collectively resisting this enclosure (and the open and covert violence around it) first behind the barricade during the clashes, then in the park, forum, neighbourhood and squat house came to define the act of being, acting, living in common. Put differently, radical democratic politics that spanned from protests in the streets and Taksim square to the occupation of Gezi Park, from forums in the neighbourhood parks to squat houses, became an alternative solidarity project rejecting to be a docile class of conservative religious consumer-citizens in favour of an anti-capitalist, self-organised, non-hierarchical, non-representative and self-sufficient community.

During the Gezi movement, squat houses in Istanbul became among the most prominent spaces where the politics of commoning could find a tangible expression. These places fostered a unique form of radical democracy, not merely theoretical but deeply connected to the shared resources and concerns of the squat's inhabitants and the neighbourhood in which it was located. The fusion of politics and space in these squat houses brought forth a practical manifestation of collective engagement and a new set of communal values around non-capitalist principles. More importantly, squat houses came to function as social centres where the 'lost feeling of community' was revived in a self-ruling, non-hierarchical social setting (Rittersberger-Tılıç, 2015: 92–93).

One such example is the Yeldeğirmeni squat house that was established in the Kadıköy district in Istanbul. The occupants of the squat connected with the residents to reclaim and re-appropriate what was stolen from the public through commodification under the AKP government. They got actively involved in the matters of the neighbourhood such as the provision of supplies for the local school or helping refugee children in the district. They also organised solidarity campaigns with the shopkeepers in the neighbourhood or created teams to help the elderly with their needs. Similar with other squatting experiences around the world (Çoban, 2015), the neighbourhood was designated as the primary unit and the centre of the common in the broader effort to transform the city (Muhalefet, 2013). Put differently, they both mobilised resources to improve the conditions of the city with a focus on local spaces, and transformed the social relations within these spaces (Ülger *et al.*, 2014). By radicalising the sphere of their everyday life (as experienced in the squares, camps and then in the park forums) the community became the source of political power. In other words, community and politics became inseparable as community became politics in/of/around the common.

## 4.5 Post-Gezi Experiences of Being/Thinking/Doing in Common

Having lived through the experience of the Gezi uprising, activists began to discuss more widely the idea of cooperatives as an alternative economic model (Öngel & Yıldırım, 2019). One example of this particular commoning practice was in 2013 when some of the workers of the Kazova textile factory took over the factory after it went bankrupt, and continued production adhering to 'auto-management' methods. But it was the food production and consumption cooperatives that became more widespread following the Gezi uprisings (Morkoç, 2018; Türkkan, 2019). The visibility of women in activism had already increased during the Gezi uprising. In the years following the demise of the movement, women-led cooperatives and other alternative economic organisations ('collectives') around the principles of solidarity economy – primarily in agricultural production and handicrafts – began to mushroom all over the country (Işıl & Değirmenci, 2020; Yerdeniz Kooperatifi, 2023). What united these and other initiatives were that they were all run by volunteers who prioritised social rather than individual good/benefit/utility, and preferred an autonomous organisational style/form in which horizontalism and consensus-oriented democratic participation in decision-making could be realised in a shared/common space (Arslantürk, 2020).

Establishment of co-working spaces as mutually shared sites of work and socialisation in Istanbul, such as the 'space on Earth' initiative, can be considered yet as another form of commoning activism that became popular in the immediate aftermath of the Gezi uprising. Although it may not appear as a movement per se, the experience itself was a peculiar response to neoliberal urbanisation and increasing precarisation in the face of soaring real estate prices in the city and deteriorating job security for freelance white-collar workers (Yeşilyurt, 2019). Aside from being merely a place of work, co-working spaces offered an 'emancipatory' potential as a non-capitalist form of work organisation. As a spatial resource, these collectives also hosted talks, workshops, film screenings, exchange bazaars, and exhibitions, all of which transformed what would otherwise be a place of capitalist production into a place of solidarity.

The 'spirit' of commoning continued to colour activism even after the waves of the Gezi uprising receded. One organisation, Deep Poverty Network, that kicked off in 2019 began mainly as a research initiative to investigate various dimensions of deepening inequalities and poverty. But when the Covid-19 pandemic hit in 2020, the network expanded its scope and became directly involved in establishing mutual care networks, establish 'to support the urgent needs of individuals who work in daily precarious jobs, who have been laid off, given unpaid leave, and living in deep poverty' (Deep Poverty Network, n.d.).

Solidarity initiatives and networks during the pandemic were not limited to poverty relief efforts. In addition to organising food delivery, initiatives such as educational support, legal help, monetary assistance to those who could not work due to curfew impositions, women's solidarity collectives, and 'neighbour outreach' efforts, among others, mushroomed following the realisation of the severity of the pandemic. Mostly relying on social media for organising and communication, various solidarity networks in different neighbourhoods and districts in Istanbul were formed (Özdemir, 2020). Some of these networks had already been established in the immediate aftermath of the Gezi protests. The pandemic served as a trigger for their reactivation. During the first days of the pandemic, volunteers were recruited who then were mobilised to reach out to different communities to determine the need, and channel resources to the needy. Some of them also connected with local administration authorities to better coordinate support efforts.

Another instance when social solidarity networks have been swiftly created and activated was the immediate aftermath of the twin earthquakes in February 2023. Miners, construction workers, heavy machinery operators, doctors and other healthcare professionals, various civil society organisations, political parties, domestic and foreign search and rescue teams, and individual volunteers all mobilised to the earthquake zone from the very first day, developing practices of 'care' that did not rely on government assistance or market logic but on a form of mobilisation of the commons (Tekin & Yükseker, 2023; also see The Care Collective, 2020). With the relief efforts and self-organised local and national collectives emerging almost instantaneously, the earthquake zone turned into a political space for bottom-up, sustainable, and human-centred encounters and practices in non-hierarchical social organising. Autonomous decision-making for more effective coordination of the relief efforts, and other acts of solidarity for building collective power were all reminiscent of the experiences during the Gezi uprising and its aftermath, from a decade ago (Ertaş, 2023).

What all these and other radical democratic examples during and following the Gezi movement demonstrate is that from within this whole experience emerged a potential and a vision for a new social order: a social order whose loose institutionalisation centred the common(s). The experience as a whole was not merely a political demand for political recognition, as radical democracy would have theorised. Nor can it be understood simply in discursive terms which would interpret it simply as building hegemony among different political demands. This radical politics as it emerged in forums and assemblies in occupied parks, neighbourhood solidarities, and squat houses turned sites of protest and creation into spaces for production and reproduction through community-oriented or community-spirited actions, and not merely an additional platform to conduct traditional politics at the local level or at multiple levels simultaneously. The whole radical democratic experience became a delicate blend of inclusiveness, plurality, a non-hierarchical structure, direct participation without pre-decided principles, and having a direct relationship with a particular physical space by way of occupying it.

It is here that the Turkish case, along with many other social movements of the twenty-first century which utilised similar radical political practices, demonstrates how the boundary between activist, organiser, volunteer, participant became blurred under these radical democratic practices. More importantly, the conventional demarcations between the social, the political, the economic and the ecological eroded for these experiences were not just anti-capitalist but also anti-systemic: their essence could not be captured neither by the capitalist logic nor its predominant and historically unrivalled alternative, socialism. As Stavrides observed, something new was materialising in these experiences: 'community-oriented or community-inspired actions that, often quite distinct from neocommunitarian, neoconservative ideologies, create or even reinvent communities in the making' (Stavrides, 2012: 586).

Once again, the idea and pursuance of the common was at the core of this community building process. It was around this emerging common that a variety of ideas, visions, and yearnings were assembled into collective actions that constituted a reworked definition of a 'social order' which did not degenerate into a narrow, homogeneous form of public (De Angelis & Harvie, 2013). More importantly, it was the 'transformation of life along anti-capitalist principles' that became the motivating and guiding principle in forums and other sites of radical democratic experimentation – a novel experimentation that could not be captured by the existing theories of radical democracy. In contrast with the ways many theorists of radical democracy confined themselves to a more conservative understanding of radicalism, activists wanted the revive what they called 'solidarity economy' where they would engage in a host of creative activism, such as closing bank accounts, encouraging shopping with local businesses and overall curbing consumption, organising 'do-it-yourself' style workshops (such as how to brew your own beer) to stop purchasing big brands, establishing exchange markets that would limit money transactions and founding or supporting non-profit cooperatives, markets and restaurants, establishing solidarity kitchens, and even using guerrilla tactics to disrupt the ordinary flow of the economy (Atılgan, 2013: 16). Overall, by rejecting the existing forms of political representation and by directly acting on ideas regarding alternative forms, contemporary social movements became a laboratory for a new social order that placed the common at the heart of a new democratic community.

## 5 Reimagining Radical Democracy and Social Movements in the Twenty-First Century

As we expressed at the beginning, *Reimagining Radical Democracy in the Global South* is a call for rethinking the ways through which 'radical democracy-as-theory' can respond to the expectations of, and demands from, 'radical democracy-as-social movement'. Our purpose is to extend an invitation to activists, academics, politicians, practitioners, policymakers, social movements groups, civil society organisations, and grassroots collectives to reimagine a more egalitarian global society reinvigorating the potential of the radical democratic paradigm. In the previous sections, we suggested that there exists a mismatch between the concept/theory of radical democracy as currently formulated in the literature and the ways it is articulated in contentious politics in non-European contexts. Social movements in Colombia and Türkiye demonstrate that new forms of political activism and emerging non-capitalist visions for a more egalitarian society challenge existing conceptual frameworks in radical democratic theory, and that a more comprehensive articulation and implementation of radical democracy beyond the narrow canvas of the Global North is urgently needed. Such an epistemological expansion is essential not only for promoting a better dialogue between theory and practice, or for highlighting the diversity of goals, methods, and motivations of contemporary social movements around the world. It is also necessary for comprehending the emancipatory potential of radical democracy in times of democratic erosion and rising authoritarianism. In other words, there is an urgent need to start rethinking radical democracy in light of the profound social changes that are happening in the twenty-first century.

## 5.1 Questions and Challenges

The current post-millennial period has presented us with numerous challenges, fluctuating from growing inequality and the rise of global poverty to environmental crises and the decline of democracy around the world. From our perspective, reimagining radical democracy in light of contemporary movements involves a nuanced understanding of current and future challenges, and a commitment to create innovative, inclusive, and sustainable solutions. By combining academic and activist perspectives around collective reflections and discussions on alternative forms of governance and innovative social orders, we believe it is possible to enrich the discourse and contribute to the development of more effective strategies towards this goal.

We also believe that the Colombian and Turkish cases open the way for tackling a number of pressing questions that still wait to be addressed: how can social movements incorporate practical intersectional perspectives to ensure inclusivity and address multiple forms of oppression? What lessons can we glean from past movements to inform our strategies for radical democracy? What insights can we derive from grassroots movements around the world? How can we foster international solidarity and collaboration to create a global movement for change inspired by radical democracy? Additionally, how can digital platforms and emerging technologies be harnessed to enhance radical democratic participation and empower marginalised voices? What potential risks and challenges are associated with their use?

While we hope that this Element will encourage new debates on these questions and others while contributing to shaping future discussions and actions that will emerge from the process of reimagining radical democracy, we are also aware that this is no easy task. Reimagining radical democracy to respond to the needs of the movements of the twenty-first century poses several challenges that demand thoughtful consideration and concerted effort. From our perspective, addressing these challenges involves a multifaceted approach that encompasses social, economic, cultural, environmental, and justice-oriented dimensions.

Regarding the economic dimension, the Turkish case illustrates the relevance and importance of imagining novel cooperative and participatory models in the realm of political economy. The challenge lies in scaling up alternative economic models including cooperatives and participatory budgeting, to counter the dominance of capitalist structures that have established themselves as if there could be no alternatives. Overcoming resistance and scepticism from established institutions and fostering the necessary infrastructure for those models is critical. In this context, rethinking radical democracy can encourage the establishment of a new form of economic democracy. Advocating for a truly 'radical' economic democracy within social movements necessitates confronting deeply entrenched power structures. This involves pushing for fair wages, workers' rights, and wealth redistribution, requiring strategic alliances and sustained efforts to influence policy changes, but more importantly, to create real alternatives to capitalism. In other words, radical democracy can be the key to reinventing a social contract in which capitalism does not play a central role in the new social order (see Varoufakis 2020 for an inspiring attempt for such formulation).

In relation to the sociocultural dimension, the challenge here lies in contesting dominant narratives and creating innovative models for cultural resilience and expression. The test, in addressing radical democratic ideas, is how to effectively utilise culturally expressive dimensions, including films, music, arts, and storytelling, to challenge prevailing narratives. This involves creating alternative platforms for cultural expression and radical democracy that can reach diverse audiences. In other words, the question is how to embrace cultural resistance mechanisms as a powerful tool for change while circumnavigating the fine line between mainstream capitalistic co-option and maintaining the grassroots authenticity of radical democracy.

Recognising and addressing the disproportionate impact of ecological challenges on marginalised communities is a complex issue that the environmental dimension aims to tackle. As the Colombian case highlights, this involves bridging the gap between environmental activism and social justice movements, ensuring inclusivity and intersectionality. Thus, integrating radical democracy into environmental justice movements requires overcoming compartmentalisation. The challenge is to accentuate the interconnectedness of social and ecological systems from a posthumanistic approach, fostering a holistic understanding that informs actionable strategies.

## 5.2 Connecting Radical Democratic Practice with Radical Democratic Theory

As *Reimagining Radical Democracy in the Global South* illustrates, environmental citizenship and practices of commoning not only offer a transformative shift from the liberal democratic interpretations of political citizenship and economic order but also inform paradigmatic innovations within the radical democratic theory. These innovations can assume various facets that reflect their positive contributions to both individual and collective subjectivities. For example, liberal democratic models typically emphasise individual rights and responsibilities within a framework of representative democracy. Citizenship in this context is often transactional, focusing on the relationship between the individual and the state, and largely confined to political participation through voting and compliance with laws. Environmental citizenship and commoning, however, extend the concept of citizenship to include collective responsibilities and the stewardship of shared resources. Thus, as we argued, environmental citizenship views citizens as active agents in environmental governance, emphasising duties towards the environment and future generations. It fosters a sense of collective responsibility and interdependence, encouraging practices that contribute to sustainability and ecological justice. This model shifts the focus from individual rights to collective well-being and the health of the planet. In the same vein, commoning is the practice of managing shared resources (commons) collectively by communities. It challenges the neoliberal emphasis on private property and individual ownership, promoting shared stewardship and collaborative management of resources such as land, water, and knowledge. This approach cultivates a sense of community and mutual aid, reshaping individuals as co-managers and co-beneficiaries of common goods.

Both environmental citizenship and commoning also invoke a fundamental transformation of subjectivity, encouraging individuals to see themselves as integral parts of a larger ecological and social system. Environmental citizenship nurtures an ecological consciousness where individuals recognise their interconnectedness with the environment. This shift in perspective encourages sustainable living practices and advocacy for policies that protect the environment. Citizens become more than just voters; they are stewards of the earth, responsible for the well-being of all living beings. At the same time, commoning fosters a deep sense of community engagement and solidarity. It requires individuals to actively participate in the governance and maintenance of commons, promoting skills such as cooperation, negotiation, and conflict resolution. This collective action transforms individuals from passive consumers to active co-creators of their social and ecological environment.

Environmental citizenship and commoning also enhance democratic participation by involving citizens directly in decision-making processes that affect their lives and communities. This direct involvement contrasts sharply with the often passive role of citizens in liberal democracies, where decision-making is largely delegated to elected representatives. Thus, environmental citizenship involves participatory governance models where citizens are directly engaged in environmental decision-making processes. This can include community-based conservation efforts, local sustainability initiatives, and participatory budgeting for environmental projects. Such engagement fosters a more inclusive and responsive form of democracy. Commoning involves the collaborative management of resources, which requires active participation and consensus-building. This democratic practice empowers individuals and communities to have a direct say in how resources should be used and maintained, fostering a sense of ownership and responsibility.

As was presented in the previous sections, both frameworks address issues of social and environmental justice more comprehensively than traditional liberal democratic models. They emphasise equity, inclusion, and the redistribution of resources, ensuring that marginalised voices are heard and that the benefits of environmental and social policies are shared equitably. Commoning practices often arise in response to the inequitable distribution of resources. By reclaiming and managing commons, communities can address social injustices and create more equitable access to essential resources. Environmental citizenship promotes policies and practices that prioritise the needs and rights of marginalised communities disproportionately affected by environmental degradation and climate change. It calls for a just transition to sustainable practices that leave no one behind.

In an era of rapid environmental and social change, the resilience and adaptability fostered by environmental citizenship and commoning are crucial. These models encourage communities to develop adaptive strategies and resilient practices that can withstand ecological and economic shocks. Environmental citizenship promotes adaptive management practices that are responsive to changing environmental conditions. This dynamic approach allows for continuous learning and adjustment, making communities more resilient to climate change and other environmental challenges. Commoning builds social capital and trust within communities, which are essential for resilience. By working together to manage the commons, communities develop strong social networks and support systems that enhance their ability to respond to crises. In other words, both environmental citizenship and commoning offer transformative pathways for radical democracy, challenging the limitations of liberal democratic models and fostering a more inclusive, participatory, and sustainable form of citizenship. By reimagining the roles and responsibilities of individuals and communities, these frameworks cultivate a deeper sense of collective identity, environmental stewardship, and social justice.

## 5.3 Learning from the Global South

There is no doubt, then, that the ways through which social movements in Colombia and Türkiye developed novel political and economic practices offer transformative lessons for a more inclusive democratic social order. Each lesson is grounded in the principles of radical democracy, emphasising the importance of diversity, participatory decision-making, imaginative institutional engagement, and long-term sustainability. The version of radical democratic theory emerging from these practices shows how actively engaging communities and promoting intersectionality can transform existing democratic arrangements. The Colombian and Turkish cases highlight the need for direct involvement of grassroots communities in decision-making processes. This inclusion fosters a richer, more diverse democratic discourse that addresses the unique needs and perspectives of these groups.

Furthermore, the intersectionality of social and environmental justice issues in Colombia and Türkiye showcases the necessity of addressing overlapping forms of oppression. Radical democratic theory can learn from this by advocating for policies and practices that recognise and address multiple, intersecting forms of marginalisation. Also, the cases of Colombia and Türkiye offer useful examples for the creation of 'from below' spaces for dialogue and collaboration, such as community assemblies and forums, which allow for the exchange of diverse experiences and ideas. These spaces enable a more participatory form of democracy where all community members can contribute to the decision-making process, as demonstrated by the inclusive practices in Colombian and Turkish movements.

Contemporary movements in Colombia and Türkiye also illustrate the power of collective action and consensus-building in dismantling hierarchical structures and the embrace of participatory decision-making processes. Both cases demonstrate how abandoning top-down decision-making in favour of horizontal, participatory structures aligns with radical democracy's emphasis on flattening hierarchies and fostering a sense of ownership and agency among participants. The success of Colombian and Turkish 'from below' assemblies and forums underscores the importance of open dialogue in building consensus and collective decision-making. Radical democratic theory can incorporate these practices to enhance participatory governance within social movements and broader democratic institutions.

Moreover, emphasising collective decision-making processes, where all members have an equal say, strengthens the democratic fabric of social movements. This approach ensures that decisions reflect the collective will and fosters a deeper commitment to democratic principles as the Colombian and Turkish cases show. It is important to remember that radical democratic theory often involves challenging existing power structures, but it also recognises the importance of strategic engagement with institutions to achieve lasting change. The cases of Colombia and Türkiye offer valuable insights into this dynamic. Both movements show that while grassroots activism is crucial, engaging with public and private institutions through lobbying, advocacy, and policy reform is equally important. Radical democracy can adopt this dual approach to maximise its impact on transforming existing institutions.

The Colombian and Turkish cases also point to the effectiveness of direct confrontation with institutions to demand reforms. Radical democratic movements can draw on these examples to advocate for systemic changes within existing institutional frameworks, thereby bridging grassroots activism and formal political engagement. Sustainable social change is a cornerstone of radical democratic theory. The Colombian and Turkish cases highlight the importance of building lasting networks and coalitions to sustain momentum.

In other words, the cases of Colombia and Türkiye provide a rich source of inspiration for advancing radical democratic theory. By emphasising inclusivity, participatory decision-making, imaginative institutional engagement, long-term sustainability, and education, these movements offer practical lessons for creating a more inclusive, equitable, and resilient democratic framework. Radical democracy can be significantly enriched by incorporating these lessons, fostering a more dynamic and transformative approach to democratic practice.

**

In conclusion, a close analysis of environmental citizenship and commoning in the cases of Colombia and Türkiye reveals possible innovative ways to revamp radical democracy as a novel epistemological and ontological framework. By delving into the intricate interplay of diverse voices and perspectives from these countries, we hope that *Reimagining Radical Democracy in the Global South* will inspire readers to reimagine radical democracy not merely as a procedural system but as a transformative force that shapes the very foundations of knowledge and existence. The new epistemological and ontological dimensions highlighted in the Element will hopefully encourage a shift in perspective, urging individuals to view radical democracy not merely as a set of institutional procedures but as a dynamic force that can shape cultural narratives and economic structures. It is our intent and expectation that the examples mentioned here will underscore that radical democracy extends beyond the political realm, influencing the core fabric of societies and offering a holistic vision for a world where power, knowledge, and existence are redefined. By engaging with the various lessons, experiences, and outcomes from both cases, we hope that scholars and activists will actively participate in the ongoing debates on and experimentations of radical democracy, fostering a global dialogue on how radical democracy can serve as a catalyst for positive change, transcending borders and envisioning a world where diversity, equality, and justice are at the forefront of societal values.

# References


Adaman, F., B. Akbulut, and U. Kocagöz. (2016). Giriş. In F. Adaman, B. Akbulut, and U. Kocagöz, eds., *Herkesin, Herkes İçin: Müşterekler Üzerine Bir Antoloji*. İstanbul: Metis Yayınları, pp. 13–23.

Akbulut, B. (2016). Sonuç. In F. Adaman, B. Akbulut, and U. Kocagöz, eds., *Herkesin, Herkes İçin: Müşterekler Üzerine Bir Antoloji*. İstanbul: Metis Yayınları, pp. 279–295.

Al-Gharbi, M. (2023). *Symbolic Capitalism: Social Justice Discourse, Inequality and the Rise of a New Elite*. Doctoral thesis, Columbia University.

Alvarez, C. (2023). Structural racism as an environmental justice issue: A multilevel analysis of the state racism index and environmental health risk from air toxics. *Journal of Racial and Ethnic Health Disparities*, **10**(1), 244–258.

Alvarez, S. (2017). *Cuerpos Gramaticales: Esculturas Vivas en la Tierra*. Barcelona: Instituto Catalán Internacional para la Paz.

Alzate Rodriguez, L. V. (2022). *Analysis of Deforestation in Colombia from the Environmental Kuznets Curve*. Bogotá: Universidad Nacional de Colombia.

Arslantürk, N. (2020). Gıda toplulukları ekseninde müştereklerimiz, müşterekçiler, dayanışma ve yeni bir ekonomi. In Ö. S. Işıl, and S. Değirmenci, eds., *Yaşamı Örgütleyen Deneyimler: Kadınlar Dayanışma Ekonomilerini ve Kooperatifleri Tartışıyor*. Ankara: Nota Bene Yayınları, pp. 307–342.

Atayurt, U. (2013). Demokratik cumhuriyetin ilk 15 günü. *Express*, **136**(July), 26–29.

Atılgan, Y. (2013). Yeniden öğrenirken. *Bir+Bir*, **24**(July–August).

Aykaç, A. (2017). *The Political Economy of Employment Relations: Alternative Theory and Practice*. New York: Routledge.

Barnett, C., and M. Low. (2009). Democracy. In A. Kobayashi, ed., *International Encyclopaedia of Human Geography*. 2nd edition. London: Elsevier, pp. 233–237.

Bauman, Z. (2007). *Liquid Times: Living in an Age of Uncertainty*. Cambridge: Polity.

Beck, U. (2002). The cosmopolitan society and its enemies. *Theory, Culture & Society*, **19**(1–2), 17–44.

Bell, K. (2016). Bread and roses: A gender perspective on environmental justice and public health. *International Journal of Environmental Research and Public Health*, **13**(10), 2–18.

Brown, W. (2019). *In the Ruins: The Rise of Anti-democratic Politics in the West*. New York: Columbia University Press.

Burke, B. (2022). *Social Exchange: Barter as Economic and Cultural Activism in Medellín, Colombia*. New Jersey: Rutgers University Press.

Calhoun, C. (1992). *Habermas and the Public Sphere*. Cambridge, MA: MIT Press.

Caniglia, B. S., R. J. Brulle, and A. Szasz. (2015). Civil society, social movements, and climate change. In R. E. Dunlap, and R. J. Brulle, eds., *Climate Change and Society: Sociological Perspectives*. New York: Oxford Academic, pp. 235–268.

Castells, M. (1997). *The Power of Identity, The Information Age: Economy, Society and Culture*, vol. II. Cambridge, MA; Oxford, UK: Blackwell. ISBN 978-1-4051-0713-6.

Castells, M. (2006). *The Network Society from Knowledge to Policy*. Washington, DC: Johns Hopkins Center for Transatlantic Relations.

Celikates, R. (2021). Radical democratic disobedience. In W. E. Scheuerman, ed., *The Cambridge Companion to Civil Disobedience*. Cambridge: Cambridge University Press, pp. 128–152.

Çoban, F. (2015). *Sokak Siyaseti: Siyasalın Gündelik Kuruluşu Bağlamında Bir İnceleme*. Istanbul: Metis Yayınları.

Çobanoğlu, Y. (2014). Türkiye'de ekolojik hareketler: yerelden evrensele (Bergama, Muğla ve Tunceli örnekleri). *Tunceli Üniversitesi Sosyal Bilimler Dergisi*, **2**(4, Spring), 105–125.

Colombia's Truth and Reconciliation Commission. (2022). *There Is Future if there is truth: Colombian Truth Commission's Final Report*. Bogotá: Colombia's Truth and Reconciliation Commission.

Comisión para el Esclarecimiento de la Verdad, la Convivencia y la No Repetición. (2022). *Convocatoria a la Paz Grande*. Bogotá: Comisión para el Esclarecimiento de la Verdad, la Convivencia y la No Repetición.

Conway, J., and J. Singh. (2011). Radical democracy in global perspective: Notes from the pluriverse. *Third World Quarterly*, **32**(4), 689–706.

Coombe, R. J., and D. Jefferson. (2021). Posthuman rights struggles and environmentalisms from below in the political ontologies of Ecuador and Colombia. *Journal of Human Rights and the Environment*, **12**(2), 177–204.

Critchley, S. (2005). True democracy. In L. Tønder, and L. Thomassen, eds., *Radical Democracy: Politics between Abundance and Lack*. Manchester: Manchester University Press, pp. 219–235.

Croucher, S. (2004). *Globalization and Belonging: The Politics of Identity in a Changing World*. Oxford: Rowman & Littlefield Press.

Dahlberg, L. (2013). Exclusions of the public sphere conception. *Journal of the European Institute for Communication and Culture*, **20**(1), 21–38.

Dahlberg, L., and E. Siapera. (2007). *Radical Democracy and the Internet: Interrogating Theory and Practice*. London: Palgrave Macmillan.

De Angelis, M. (2010). The production of commons and the 'explosion' of the middle class. *Antipode*, **42**(4), 954–977.

De Angelis, M., and Harvie, D. (2013). The commons. In M. Parker, G. Cheney, V. Fournier, and C. Land, eds., *The Routledge Companion to Alternative Organization*. New York: Routledge, pp. 280–294.

Deep Poverty Network. (n.d.). Who Are We? Deep Poverty Network (blog). https://derinyoksullukagi.org/en/who-are-we/ [Last Accessed: 1 September 2023].

Del Lucchese, F. (2016). Spinoza and constituent power. *Contemporary Political Theory*, **15**(2), 182–204.

Dhaliwal, A. (1996). Can the subaltern vote? In D. Trend, ed., *Radical Democracy Identity, Citizenship and the State*. New York: Routledge, pp. 42–61.

Dobson, A. (2004). *Citizenship and the Environment*. Oxford: Oxford University Press.

Domaneschi, L. (2019). The sociomateriality of cooking: The practice turn in contemporary food studies. *Sociologica*, **13**(3), 119–133.

Duru, B. (2013). Demokratik, ekolojik yerel yönetimlere ulaşmada köyler ve köy kanunu'nun taşıdığı olanaklar. *Birikim*, **296**, 55–63.

Duru, B. (2018). What are the commons? On natural, urban, social commons and their effects on urban social movements. In E. Erdoğan, N. Yüce, and Ö. Özbay, eds., *The Politics of the Commons: From Theory to Struggle*. Istanbul: Sivil ve Ekolojik Haklar Derneği (SEHAK), pp. 11–28.

Elliott, D. and D. C. Esty. (2023). Environmental law for the 21st century: CSAS Working Paper 23–05. *Pace Environmental Law Review*, **40**(3), 3–62.

EPM – Empresas Públicas de Medellin. (2007). *Informe Anual 2007: Responsabilidad Social Empresarial*. Medellin: EPM.

Ercan-Bilgiç, E., and Z. Kafkaslı. (2013). *Gencim, özgürlükçüyüm, ne istiyorum? ##direngeziparkı Anketi Sonuç Raporu*. Istanbul: Istanbul Bilgi University.

Ertaş, D. (2023). Reclaiming space: The legacy of Gezi and the struggle for post-disaster planning in Türkiye. *Jadaliyya*, 6 July. www.jadaliyya.com/Details/45185 [Last Accessed: 17 December 2023].

Estrada, A. (2010). Del dolor a la propuesta: Voces del panel de víctimas. *Revista de Estudios Sociales*, **36**, 114–125.

Falk, R. (1994). The making of global citizenship. In B. van Steenbergen, ed., *The Condition of Citizenship*. London: Sage, pp. 27–140.

Fırat, B. Ö. (2018). Global movement cycles and commoning movements. In E. Erdoğan, N. Yüce, and Ö. Özbay, eds., *The Politics of the Commons: From Theory to Struggle*. Istanbul: Sivil ve Ekolojik Haklar Derneği (SEHAK), pp. 66–79.

Fırat, B. Ö. (2022). A double movement of enclosure and commons: Commoning emek movie theatre in three acts. *City*, **26**(5–6), 1029–1044.

Forst, R. (2017). *Normativity and Power: Analysing Social Orders of Justification*. Oxford: Oxford University Press.

Fraser, N. (1996). Equality, difference and radical democracy. In D. Trend, ed., *Radical Democracy Identity, Citizenship and the State*. New York: Routledge, pp. 197–208.

Fraser, N. (2020). *The Old Is Dying and the New Cannot Be Born*. London: Verso Books.

Fraser, N. (2022). *Cannibal Capitalism: How Our System Is Devouring Democracy, Care, and the Planet – and What We Can Do about It*. London: Verso Books.

Freeden, M. (2003). *Ideology: A Very Short Introduction*. Oxford: Oxford University Press.

Front Line Defenders. (2019). *Global Analysis 2019*. Dublin: Front Line Defenders.

Front Line Defenders. (2023). *#COLOMBIA*. Dublin: Front Line Defenders.

García de la Torrc, C. I., and C. I. Aramburo Siegert. (2011). *Geografías de la Guerra, El Poder y La Resistencia. Oriente y Urabá Antioqueños 1990–2008*. Bogotá: CINEP.

Genç, F. (2018). Urban social movements and the politics of the commons in Istanbul. In E. Erdoğan, N. Yüce, and Ö. Özbay, eds., *The Politics of the Commons: From Theory to Struggle*. Istanbul: Sivil ve Ekolojik Haklar Derneği (SEHAK), pp. 80–98.

Global Witness. (2012). *Annual Review 2012: Exposing Hidden Interests*. London: Global Witness.

Global Witness. (2022). *Annual Report 2022: Rising to the Challenge of a World in Crisis*. London: Global Witness.

Goodman, J. (2017, March 29). *Social Movement Participation and Climate Change. Oxford Research Encyclopedia of Climate Science*. https://oxfordre.com/climatescience/view/10.1093/acrefore/9780190228620.001.0001/acrefore-9780190228620-e-340 [Last Accessed: 23 September 2024].

Guerrero, L. M. (2010). *Historia del Movimiento Ambiental Departamento de Risaralda Aportes, conceptos, prácticas sociales de la cultura ambiental y la participación social*. Pereira: Universidad Tecnológica de Pereira.

Güven, E. (2013). Hayat barikatta o'lum. *Tempo*, **54**(July), 76–81.

Habermas, J. (1994). Three normative models of democracy. *Constellations*, **1** (1), 1–10.

Habermas, J. (1997). Modernity: An unfinished project. In M. P. Entrèves, and S. Benhabib, eds., *Habermas and the Unfinished Project of Modernity: Critical Essays on the Philosophical Discourse of Modernity*. Cambridge, MA: MIT Press, pp. 38–59.

Hadjichambis, A. Ch., and P. Reis. (2020). Introduction to the conceptualisation of environmental citizenship for twenty-first-century education. In A. Ch. Hadjichambis, Pedro Reis, Demetra Paraskeva-Hadjichambi, *et al.*, eds., *Conceptualizing Environmental Citizenship for 21st Century Education*. Environmental Discourses in Science Education, vol. 4. London: Springer, pp. 1–14.

Hardt, M., and A. Negri. (2017). *Assembly*. New York: Oxford University Press.

Hazar-Kalonya, D. (2021). Environmental movements in Türkiye from the perspective of commons. *International Journal of the Commons*, **15**(1), 236–258.

Held, D. (2004). *A Globalizing World? Culture, Economics, Politics*. London: Routledge.

Hermes, J. (2006). Citizenship in the age of the internet. *European Journal of Communication*, **21**(3), 295–309.

Howarth, D., and K. Roussos. (2022). Radical democracy, the commons and everyday struggles during the Greek crisis. *The British Journal of Politics and International Relations*, **25**(2), 311–327.

Ibrahim, Y. (2021). *Posthuman Capitalism: Dancing with Data in the Digital Economy*. London: Routledge.

Illouz, E. (2007). *Cold Intimacies: The Making of Emotional Capitalism*. London: Polity.

Işıl, Ö. S., and S. Değirmenci (eds.). (2020). *Yaşamı Örgütleyen Deneyimler: Kadınlar Dayanışma Ekonomilerini ve Kooperatifleri Tartışıyor*. Ankara: Nota Bene Yayınları, pp. 89–114.

Isin, E. (2008). Theorizing acts of citizenship. In E. Isin, and G. Nielsen, eds., *Acts of Citizenship*. London: Palgrave Macmillan, pp. 15–43.

Jean-Louis, L. (2023). *The Solidarity Economy*. Minnesota: University of Minnesota Press.

Kalyvas, A. (2005). Popular sovereignty, democracy, and the constituent power. *Constellations*, **12**(2), 223–244.

Kawano, E. (2020). Solidarity economy: Building an economy for people & planet. *Solidarity Economy Association*, www.solidarityeconomy.coop/wp-content/uploads/2017/06/Kawano-E.-2018_Solidarity-Economy.pdf [Last Accessed: 17 December 2023].

Kawano, E., T. N. Masterson, and J. Teller-Elsberg. (2010). *Solidarity Economy I: Building Alternatives for People and Planet*. Amherst, MA: Center for Popular Economics.

Kibar, S., and Tatari, B. (2013). Birkaç ağaç, her türlü insan. *Tempo*, **54**(July), 62–71.

Kioupkiolis, A., and G. Katsambekis (eds.). (2014). *Radical Democracy and Collective Movements Today*. Burlington: Ashgate.

Klein, N. (2017). How power profits from disaster. *The Guardian*, 6 July. www.theguardian.com/us-news/2017/jul/06/naomi-klein-how-power-profits-from-disaster [Last Accessed: 17 December 2023].

Konda Araştırma ve Danışmanlık (Konda). (2014). Gezi Raporu. https://konda.com.tr/rapor/67/gezi-raporu [Last Accessed: 17 December 2023].

Konings, M. (2016). Governing the system: Risk, finance, and neoliberal reason. *European Journal of International Relations*, **22**(2), 268–288.

Laclau, E. (2005). *On Populist Reason*. London: Verso Books.

Laclau, E., and C. Mouffe. (1985). *Hegemony and Socialist Strategy: Towards a Radical Democratic Politics*. London: Verso.

Laville, J.-L. (2023). *The Solidarity Economy*. Minnesota: University of Minnesota Press.

Little, A., and M. Lloyd (eds.). (2008). *The Politics of Radical Democracy*. Edinburgh: Edinburgh University Press.

Llano-Arias, V. (2014). *Communication Practices and Citizens' Participation in the Colombian Water Movement*. PhD Thesis. Dublin: University College Dublin.

Lyon, D. (2020). *Pandemic Surveillance*. London: Polity.

Marable, M. (1996). A new American socialism? In D. Trend, ed., *Radical Democracy Identity, Citizenship and the State*. New York: Routledge, pp. 146–156.

Marchart, O. (2007). *Post-Foundational Political Thought: Political Difference in Nancy, Lefort, Badiou and Laclau*. Edinburgh: Edinburgh University Press.

Mashallah Team. (2013). Gezi park occupation (liveblog). 9 June. *Mashallah News*. www.mashallahnews.com/gezi-park-occupation-liveblog/ [Last Accessed: 17 December 2023].

Mason, P. (2015). *Postcapitalism: A Guide to Our Future*. London: Penguin.

Matijasevich, D. (2019). *Radical Democracy and Its Limits*. London: Palgrave MacMillan.

Mazzocchi, F. (2020). A deeper meaning of sustainability: Insights from indigenous knowledge. *The Anthropocene Review*, **7**(1), 77–93.

Melo Parra, J. P. (2018). Vínculo entre la constitución cultural y la constitución ecológica. In A. Garcia, ed., *La Corte Ambiental: Expresiones Ciudadanas Sobre Los Avances Constitucionales*. Bogotá: Fundación Heinrich Böll, pp. 279–298.

Monro, S. (2012). Sexuality, space and intersectionality: the case of LGB equalities in UK local government. In: *5th International Conference on Equality, Diversity and Inclusion, 23rd–25th July 2012, Toulouse, France.*

Morkoç, T. (2018). Krize karşı: kooperatifler ve komünler. *Gazete Duvar*, 12 August. www.gazeteduvar.com.tr/ekonomi/2018/12/08/krize-karsi-kooperatifler-ve-komunler [Last Accessed: 17 December 2023].

Mouffe, C. (1993). *The Return of the Political*. London: Verso Books.

Mouffe, C. (1996). Radical democracy or liberal democracy? In D. Trend, ed., *Radical Democracy Identity, Citizenship and the State*. New York: Routledge, pp. 19–26.

Mouffe, C. (2000). *The Democratic Paradox*. London: Verso Books.

Mouffe, C. (2005). *On the Political*. Abingdon: Routledge.

Mouffe, C. (2013). *Agonistics: Thinking the World Politically*. London: Verso Books.

Mouffe, C. (2018). *For a Left Populism*. London: Verso Books.

Muhalefet. (2013). Yeldeğirmeni işgal evinde yeni bir yaşam kuruluyor. 6 December. https://muhalefet.org/haber-yeldegirmeni-isgal-evinde-yeni-bir-yasam-kuruluyor-51-8827.aspx [Last Accessed: 17 December 2023].

Murillo-Sandoval, P. J., J. Kilbride, E. Tellman, *et al.* (2023). The post-conflict expansion of coca farming and illicit cattle ranching in Colombia. *Scientific Reports*, (13), 19–65.

NCHM – The National Centre of Historical Memory of Colombia. (2018). *Sujetos victimizados y daños causados: Balance de la contribución del CNMH al esclarecimiento histórico*. Bogotá: Colombian National Press.

NCHM – The National Centre of Historical Memory of Colombia. (2019). *Análisis cuantitativo del paramilitarismo en Colombia*. Bogotá: Colombian National Press.

Newman, S. (2014). Occupy and autonomous political life. In A. Kioupkiolis, and G. Katsambekis, eds., *Radical Democracy and Collective Movements Today*. Burlington: Ashgate, pp. 93–110.

Newman, S. (2016). Occupy and autonomous political life. In A. Kioupkiolis and G. Katsambekis, eds., *Radical Democracy and Collective Movements Today: The Biopolitics of the Multitude versus the Hegemony of the People*. London: Routledge, pp. 93–110.

Ní Mhurchú, A. (2014). Citizenship beyond state sovereignty. In E. Isin, and P. Nyers, eds., *Routledge Handbook of Global Citizenship Studies*. London: Routledge, pp. 119–127

North, P., and M. Cato. (2017). *Towards Just and Sustainable Economies the Social and Solidarity Economy North and South*. Bristol: Bristol University Press.

Nykvist, B., and J. von Heland. (2014). Social-ecological memory as a source of general and specified resilience. *Ecology and Society*, **19**(2), 47–61.

Omi, M., and H. Winant. (1996). Imagine there's no heaven. In D. Trend, ed., *Radical Democracy Identity, Citizenship and the State*. New York: Routledge, pp. 157–164.

Öngel, F. S., and U. D. Yıldırım (eds.). (2019). *Krize Karşı Kooperatifler: Deneyimler-Tartışmalar-Alternatifler*. Ankara: NotaBene Yayınları.

Özdemir, S. (2020). 'Capitalism kills, solidarity gives life': A glimpse of solidarity networks in Türkiye. In M. Sitrin, and C. Sembrar, eds., *Pandemic Solidarity: Mutual Aid During the Covid-19 Crisis*. London: Pluto Press, pp. 18–34.

Pettit, P. (2013). *On the People's Terms: A Republican Theory and Model of Democracy*. Cambridge: Cambridge University Press.

Plummer, K. (2003). *Intimate Citizenship: Private Decisions and Public Dialogues*. Seattle: University of Washington Press.

Popp-Madsen, B. A. (2022). Non-domination and constituent power: Socialist republicanism versus radical democracy. *Philosophy & Social Criticism*, **49** (10), 1182–1199.

Poulain, J.-P. (2005). *Sociologías de la alimentación. Los comensales y el espacio social alimentario.* Madrid: Editorial UOC.

Pugh, M. (2008). *State and Society: A Social and Political History of Britain since 1870*. London: Bloomsbury Academic.

Ramírez, A. (2023). *Ecología integral: una mirada sistémica de cara a la problemática ambiental actual*. Bogotá: Editorial Pontificia Universidad Javeriana.

Rancière, J. (1999). *Dis-agreement: Politics and Philosophy.* Minnesota: University of Minnesota Press.

Red, Cross (2018). *Humanitarian Challenges 2018: ICRC Colombia Report.* Bogotá: Red Cross Press.

Republic of Colombia. (1993). Law 99 of 1993: Establishing the Ministry of Environment, reorganizing the public sector responsible for managing and conserving the environment and renewable natural resources, and organizing the National Environmental System (SINA). Official Gazette No. 41.146, 22 December, 1993.

Rey-Araújo, P. M. (2021). *Capitalism, Institutions and Social Orders*. New York: Routledge.

Richardson, W., and J. A. McNeish. (2021). Granting rights to rivers in Colombia significance for extrACTIVISM and governance. In J. Shapiro, and J. A. McNeish, eds., *Our Extractive Age Expressions of Violence and Resistance*. London: Routledge, pp. 155–176.

Rittersberger-Tılıç, H. (2015). Squatting (in Türkiye): A practice of transforming public spaces into Commons? In N. Konak, and R. Ö. Dönmez, eds., *Waves of Social Movement Mobilizations in the Twenty-First Century: Challenges to the Neo-Liberal World Order and Democracy*. Lanham, MD: Lexington Books, pp. 83–99.

Roa, M. C. (2016). Environmental democratization and water justice in extractive frontiers of Colombia. *Geoforum*, **85**, 58–71.

Robinson, A., and S. Tormey. (2009). Is 'another world' possible? Laclau, Mouffe and social movements. In A. Little, and M. Lloyd, eds., *The Politics of Radical Democracy*. Edinburgh: Edinburgh University Press, pp. 133–157.

Robinson, C. (1983). *Black Marxism: The Making of the Black Radical Tradition*. Chapel Hill: The University of North Carolina Press.

Roelvink, G., K. St. Martin, and J. K. Gibson-Graham. (2015). *Making Other Worlds Possible: Performing Diverse Economies*. Minnesota: University of Minnesota Press.

Sassen, S. (2007). *Una sociología de la globalización*. Barcelona: Katz.

Scheidel, A., D. Del Bene, and J. Liu. (2020). Environmental conflicts and defenders: A global overview. *Global Environmental Change*, **63**, 1–12.

Schwiertz, H. (2021). Political subjectivation and the in/visible politics of migrant youth organizing in Germany and the United States. *International Political Sociology*, **15**(3), 397–414.

Schwiertz, H. (2022). Radical democratic theory and migration: The Refugee Protest March as a democratic practice. *Philosophy & Social Criticism*, **48** (2), 89–309.

Smart, B. (1994). Digesting the modern diet: Gastro-porn, fast food, and panic eating. In K. Tester, ed., *The Flaneur*. London: Routledge, pp. 158–180.

Speth, J., and K. Courrier. (2020). *The New Systems Reader Alternatives to a Failed Economy*. New York: Routledge.

Srnicek, N. (2017). *Platform Capitalism*. Cambridge: Polity.

Stammen, L., and M. Meissner. (2022). Social movements' transformative climate change communication: Extinction rebellion's artivism. *Social Movement Studies*, published online. https://doi.org/10.1080/14742837.2022.2122949.

Stavrides, S. (2012). Squares in movement. *South Atlantic Quarterly*, **111**(3), 585–596.

Stavrides, S. (2020). Life as commons. *Undisciplined Environments*. 8 May. https://undisciplinedenvironments.org/2020/05/08/life-as-commons/ [Last Accessed: 17 December 2023].

Stevenson, N. (2003). *Cultural Citizenship: Cosmopolitan Questions*. Milton Keynes: Open University Press.

Sutton, P. (2019). *Explaining Environmentalism: In Search of a New Social Movement*. London: Routledge.

Tamayo Gomez, C. (2012). Communicative citizenship, preliminary approaches. *Signo y Pensamiento*, **31**(60),106–128.

Tamayo Gomez, C. (2017). Communicative citizenship and human rights from a transnational perspective: Social movements of victims of Eastern Antioquia, Colombia. *Emulations – Revue de sciences sociales*, **19**, 25–49.

Tamayo Gomez, C. (2022). Recognition as transitional justice 'from below': Analysing victims' grassroots activism in postconflict Colombia. *The International Journal of Transitional Justice*, **16**(3), 314–330.

Tamayo Gomez, C. (2023). Understanding victims' narratives as actions of social disobedience in transitional justice times: The case of the Never Again museum in Colombia. In L. Daher, ed., *Democratic Protests and New Forms of Collective Action: When Disobedience Is Social*. Cham: Springer, pp. 103–115.

Tambakaki, P. (2019). Rethinking radical democracy. *Contemporary Political Theory*, **18**(4), 498–518.

Tarazona-Pedraza, A. (2010). Movimiento en defensa del Lago de la Cocha, Pasto, Nariño, Colombia (1993–2001). *Luna Azul*, **30**, 108–141.

Tekin, U., and D. Yükseker. (2023). Deprem sonrasında yeni bir toplumsallık: umursamazlık mı, dayanışma mı? *Aposto*, 26 February. https://aposto.com/s/deprem-sonrasinda-yeni-bir-toplumsallik [Last Accessed: 17 December 2023].

The Care Collective. (2020). *The Care Manifesto: The Politics of Interdependence*. London : Verso.

Tilly, C. (1995). *Popular Contention in Great Britain, 1758–1834*. Cambridge, MA: Harvard University Press.

Tobasura-Acuña, I. (2007). Ambientalismos y ambientalistas: una expresión del ambientalismo en Colombia. *Ambiente & Sociedade*, **X**(2), 45–60.

Tønder, L., and L. Thomassen. (2005). Introduction: Rethinking radical democracy between abundance and lack. In L. Tønder, and L. Thomassen, eds., *Radical Democracy: Politics between Abundance and Lack*. Manchester: Manchester University Press, pp. 1–13.

Trend, D. (ed.). (1996a). *Radical Democracy: Identity, Citizenship, and the State*. New York: Routledge.

Trend, D. (1996b). Democracy's crisis of meaning. In D. Trend, ed., *Radical Democracy Identity, Citizenship and the State*. New York: Routledge, pp. 7–18.

Türkkan, S. (2019). Vintage modası şimdi gıda kooperatiflerinde: 'yeni bir iletişim yolu buluyoruz'. *Saha Dergisi*, **5**(January), 76–83. https://hyd.org.tr/attachments/article/510/saha5.pdf [Last Accessed: 17 December 2023].

Ülger, Z., E. Sandıkçı, B. Yoldaş, and Ş. Akın. (2014). Kadıköy'de bir hayalet dolaşıyor: yeldeğirmeni dayanışması. *Redaksiyon*, **8**(May).

Uluğ, Ö. M., and Y. G. Acar. (2014). *Bir Olmadan Biz Olmak*. Ankara: Dipnot Yayınları.

UNDP – United Nations Development Programme. (2010). *Oriente Antioqueño: Análisis de la conflictividad*. Bogotá: United Nations Development Programme Press.

Utting, P. (2015). *Social and Solidarity Economy: Beyond the Fringe?* London: Zed Books.

Valencia, S. (2018). *Gore Capitalism*. Cambridge, MA: MIT Press.

Varoufakis, Y. (2020). *Another Now: Dispatches from an Alternative Present*. London: Bodley Head.

Vertovec, S. (2009). *Transnationalism*. London: Routledge.

Volk, C. (2021). On a radical democratic theory of political protest: Potentials and shortcomings. *Critical Review of International Social and Political Philosophy*, **24**(4), 437–459.

Wolf, N. (2022). *The Bodies of Others: The New Authoritarians, Covid-19 and the War against the Human*. London: All Seasons Press.

Wright, E. O. (2010). *Envisioning Real Utopias*. London: Verso.

WWF – World Wide Fund For Nature. (2023). *Forest Pathways Report 2023*. London: WWF.

Yazıcı, G., and B. Ö. Fırat. (2013). Hepimiz İştirakçiyiz. *Express*, **139**(November–December).

Yerdeniz Kooperatifi. (2023). Gezi'den kooperatiflere bir dayanışma ekonomisi örgütlenme deneyimi. *Jadaliyya*, 6 July. www.jadaliyya.com/Details/45184 [Last Accessed: 17 December 2023].

Yeşilyurt, A. (2019). Bir müşterek olarak dünyada mekân deneyimi: 'herkes için ama hiç kimsenin de.' *Praksis*, **1**(49), 67–82.

Zaretsky, E. (1996). Identity and democracy: A critical perspective. In D. Trend, ed., *Radical Democracy Identity, Citizenship and the State*. New York: Routledge, pp. 140–145.

Zitcer, A. (2021). *Practising Cooperation: Mutual Aid beyond Capitalism*. Minnesota: University of Minnesota Press.

Žižek, S. (2008). *The Plague of Fantasies*. New York: Verso.

Žižek, S. (2018). *Like a Thief in Broad Daylight: Power in the Era of Post-Humanity*. London: Allen Lane.

Žižek, S. (2019). *The Relevance of the Communist Manifesto*. London: Polity.

Zuboff, S. (2019). *The Age of Surveillance Capitalism Book*. London: Profile Books.

# Acknowledgements

We would like to express our gratitude to the two anonymous reviewers whose constructive comments contributed to the improvement of the Element. Any remaining errors or shortcomings in the text are solely ours. We are also grateful to the British Academy for providing a generous fellowship to support this project in 2023. Finally, we would like to acknowledge the Parkinson Building at the University of Leeds and Leeds Central Library which became a sanctuary for us during the summer of 2023 when the bulk of the Element was written.

## Cambridge Elements

# Comparative Political Theory

Leigh K. Jenco
*London School of Economics*

Leigh K. Jenco (PhD, Chicago) works across the disciplinary platforms of political theory, intellectual history, and East Asian studies. She is the author of *Changing Referents: Learning Across Space and Time in China and the West* (Oxford, 2015) and has published articles in the *American Political Science Review, Journal of Asian Studies, Modern China,* and *Political Theory.*

## About the Series

Responding to urgent concerns as well as analyzing long-standing issues, the Comparative Political Theory Elements series invites engagements with texts and media from multiple languages, genres, and time periods. Elements in this series demonstrate the viability and meaning of historically-marginalized bodies of thought for audiences beyond their place of origin, while maintaining attention to the rich particularity of diverse global reflections on politics.

**Cambridge Elements** ☰

# Comparative Political Theory

---

Elements in the Series

*Settlers in Indian Country*
Charles W. A. Prior

*Maimonides and Jewish Theocracy: The Human Hand of Divine Rule*
Charles H. T. Lesch

*The Pluralistic Frameworks of Ibn Rushd and Abdullahi Ahmed An-Na'im*
Ayesha Omar

*Reimagining Radical Democracy in the Global South: Emerging Paradigms from Colombia and Türkiye*
Kaan Ağartan and Camilo Tamayo Gomez

A full series listing is available at: www.cambridge.org/ECPT

For EU product safety concerns, contact us at Calle de José Abascal, 56–1°, 28003 Madrid, Spain or eugpsr@cambridge.org.

www.ingramcontent.com/pod-product-compliance
Ingram Content Group UK Ltd.
Pitfield, Milton Keynes, MK11 3LW, UK
UKHW022144080726
473066UK00010B/752
*9781009498524*